26-7-3-13
George
Leftwich

A Conscript
In Kansas

Neville
Williams
Cadet 20

A Conscript in Korea

A Conscript in Korea

Neville Williams

Pen & Sword
MILITARY

First published in Great Britain in 2009 by
Pen & Sword Military
an imprint of
Pen & Sword Books Ltd
47 Church Street
Barnsley
South Yorkshire
S70 2AS

ISBN 978 1 84884 131 4

A CIP catalogue record for this book is available from the British Library.

Printed and bound in the UK
by CPI Antony Rowe, Chippenham, Wiltshire

Pen & Sword Books Ltd incorporates the imprints of
Pen & Sword Aviation, Pen & Sword Maritime, Pen & Sword Military,
Wharncliffe Local History, Pen and Sword Select, Pen and Sword
Military Classics, Leo Cooper, Remember When,
Seaforth Publishing and Frontline Publishing.

For a complete list of Pen & Sword titles please contact
PEN & SWORD BOOKS LIMITED
47 Church Street, Barnsley, South Yorkshire, S70 2AS, England
E-mail: enquiries@pen-and-sword.co.uk
Website: www.pen-and-sword.co.uk

Contents

Contents

Maps

Acknowledgements

My thanks to my son Neil for his work on the illustrations, and to Christine Foley Secretarial Services.

Chapter 1

The Imperial War Museum, London

In July 2000, I was travelling by train to a small town in Switzerland called Engelberg. My wife and I were enjoying a lovely holiday based in Lucerne, but on this particular day we were travelling to Engelberg in order to take the cable car which would transport us to the top of the 10,000ft Mount Titlis. The sky was a brilliant blue, the scenery was magnificent and it truly was one of those days when you felt that God was in his heaven and all was right with the world.

Sitting across from my wife and I was a middle-aged man and a slightly younger lady who, it transpired, was his wife. The gentleman, a Korean, spoke very good English and we soon struck up a pleasant conversation. He was, apparently, an engineer who specialized in the manufacture and sale of mountain bikes, and was in Europe to promote his product. I was a retired engineer who had spent some forty-eight years in the same profession working for a number of different companies.

At one point I mentioned that I had been in his country between 1951 and 1952 as a young 21-year-old National Serviceman, fighting in the Korean War. To my utter amazement, he seemed almost startled by this revelation and immediately jumped up and started shaking my hand vigorously. 'Thank you,' he said, 'for helping to save my country.' He then spoke in a very animated fashion to his wife, and she also got up and shook my hand.

He went on to explain that his wife had been only two years old when the war broke out but that he had been eight. He continued, telling me what a marvellous standard of living they now had, and all because of the sacrifices our boys had made. Both he and his wife had been able to get a university education which would never have been possible under the oppressive communist regime. How strange life can be! There was I sitting in a train in Switzerland, being thanked by a Korean engineer and his wife, for something I had done forty-nine years earlier.

When, as a young National Serviceman, I had been shipped out to

Korea in 1951, I didn't know, without reference to a map, exactly where the country was and, like many others, I was not very sure why this particular war was being fought. Was it some kind of stand against communism or was it to protect the vast mineral deposits embedded in this lonely, isolated, mountainous country – or was it the prelude to a much larger conflict? Perhaps it was a trial of strength by the East and West, being carried out on what might be called neutral ground. I think it was of some significance that when we got out there and started digging trenches and dugouts, we often came across seams of minerals. Whatever the reasons, once we were in the theatre of war, ours was not to reason why – ours was to do or die, as they say!

The Korean people at that time were not a warlike nation. Rather, they were mild mannered, gentle and honest who, by and large, did not really understand what the war was about, except that they were trapped right in the middle of it. Not many years before they had been under the oppressive yoke of the Japanese and now here they were again, fighting for their very existence.

The Republic of Korea (ROK) Army, of course, was a different kettle of fish, being made of up of tough fighters who feared no one, but it was small in number and they could not have held back the tide of communism on their own.

That chance meeting in Switzerland sent my mind racing back over the years, but in the week when we returned home, an even more remarkable event took place, which caused me to put pen to paper and write this account of my National Service training which culminated in my spending twelve months on active service in the Korean War. Whilst many features of war are common to everyone involved, it is a fact that each individual in a conflict has a unique experience which becomes indelibly imprinted on that person's memory. The narrative which I have now recorded is based on my own personal memories, experiences, feelings and thoughts when, as a young conscript, I was thrust into a war which I did not really understand, and did not really care about. The Korean War was often called 'the forgotten war' as indeed it was, except of course for those involved. That handshake in Switzerland helped to convince me that, as far as any war can be, the Korean War was a just war and one that had to be fought to stop the spread of that evil, faithless, Godless, doctrine – 'communism'.

As history has shown Russian-type communism requires fear and repression to make it work, but in the long run, these destructive forces cause it to crumble from within. The Chinese, however, have moulded their brand of communism to fit their ancient way of life and, it seems to me, that the Chinese Government has developed a system which is a cross between an autocratic emperor and a few communistic-type ideologies, plus a little flavouring of democracy. Their ability to work hard, plus their innate craft skills, has made it one of, if not the, most powerful nation on earth. The peace which Korea now enjoys was bought at a heavy price, both for the Americans, the United Nations troops involved and the Koreans themselves, not to mention the thousands of Chinese who must have died. In the Welch Regiment alone, of which I was part, thirty-two men were killed and over one hundred wounded. There were also many other types of ill-health and injury. We, who are fortunate enough to survive this life to a good age in reasonable health, are indeed blessed, but there is something immensely sad about the loss of young people who are in the prime of their life.

One week after returning from our holiday in Switzerland, my wife and I decided to go and see the Holocaust Exhibition at the Imperial War Museum in London, that sombre reminder of the rise to power of the Nazi Party, and the subsequent slaughter of millions of Jews, gave a rare insight into the minds of the men who conceived and carried out these barbaric and evil acts.

However, on leaving that particular part of the museum we strolled into the section marked 'Wars since 1945'. Eventually we came to the section on Korea and whilst we were looking there my wife suddenly called out, 'Look Nev, you're in one of the pictures!' To my surprise there I was standing by a jeep along with one soldier from each of the Commonwealth battalions in the Commonwealth Division. A very odd combination you might think, but thereby hangs a tale. I had known of this photograph, and had even been promised a copy by the divisional padre who was attached to the Division in Korea, but had never received one. The story behind this photograph I can now relate.

In the summer of 1952 I had been in Korea some eight months or so, and on the day in question I was busy digging a bunker when the Regimental Sergeant Major (RSM) arrived on site, told me to drop everything and follow him.

'Come on, Corporal Williams,' he said, 'the CO wants to see you.' He didn't even give me time to put my shirt on, believe it or not. What a strange circumstance!

Into his jeep we went and in no time at all I was in our HQ area standing to attention in the CO's bunker. As I stood there the CO eyed me up and down with an amused look on his face, before snapping out, 'OK, RSM, he'll be OK. Get him kitted out.'

What was it all about, I thought, unable to get a handle on this unusual situation? Once outside I quite naturally asked the RSM what it was all about, but he was obviously under starter's order to keep mum.

Next I was bundled into a jeep and off we went to one of our supply echelons where I was duly kitted out with a completely new summer kit: shirt, lightweight trousers, belt, putties, boots, hat and a new slip-on Commonwealth armband with stripe and flash. I even got new underwear and since there were no mannequin parades in Korea I really did wonder.

In no time at all we were back in the jeep zigzagging down the bulldozed roads to where I could not guess. After about half an hour we stopped for something to eat at a reserve centre, and since they had a dammed-up stream which made a very serviceable swimming pool, I decided to have a quick dip. To my surprise who should I meet in this pool but one of my old barrack-room mates from my days in D Company – Ishline Hughes.

Poor Ishline, his situation was anything but a happy one, although truth to say he seemed to be his usual cheery self. Even though he was being allowed a swim, he was in fact under close arrest, and was en route to face a court martial. His offence was officially recorded as 'sleeping on guard', but what had really happened was that whilst he was on guard duty one morning just before stand down, he had put his head under his poncho (three-quarter cape) to have a swig of beer, which was available from time to time when NAAFI supplies were sent up to the line.

However, on this occasion a very unusual occurrence took place in that a brigadier arrived on site and decided to tour the trenches. It was raining at the time and another few minutes would have seen Ishline stood down, but as it was the Brigadier stumbled across him under his poncho. The fact that it was a clear morning made no difference and poor Ishline was immediately arrested and charged. Unfortunately for Ishline his training record was not good, because he was a very spirited lad who sometimes played the NCOs up a bit. This had landed him with a few sessions of 'jankers' whilst in the UK, so that while his active service record was good, his total record on paper looked bad. His CO spoke well of him regarding his active service, but it was to be of no avail, and I heard later that he got twelve months detention.

His work on patrols had more than proved his worth, but a private versus a brigadier is a no-contest situation. It was also said at the time that he would have to do an extra year's National Service, but I never saw him again so I never found out if this was the case. Chatting to Ishline in the pool at that time, I could see that he was resigned to his fate whatever it might be, but I was convinced he would take it all in his stride once he knew what the sentence was.

This was the same National Serviceman who once ran past me in the barracks with an MP jankers corporal close on his heels telling him to move it! Yet in spite of doing everything at the double he could still whisper out of the corner of his mouth, 'The poor old Corporal's having a job to keep up.' As I left the pool I wished him well, but I couldn't help thinking what a waste of a good soldier. In spite of his roguishness, I would have been glad to have him on my side, especially in a tight corner.

I quickly dressed, and the RSM and I were soon speeding towards our destination, wherever that might be. Eventually we reached what looked like an HQ site. Plenty of notices, plenty of brass and a very large parade ground, bulldozed flat for purpose, which was something I hadn't seen since leaving the UK. As we got out of the jeep we were greeted by a sergeant, who led us away to a parked jeep, around which was one soldier from each battalion in the Commonwealth Division. Now I understood! It was a photograph session – but why?

We weren't kept guessing for long as none other than General Cassells, who commanded the Division, suddenly appeared, grinning all over his face. In the immediate future he was due to hand over to someone else and he wanted a souvenir photograph with one man from each regiment stood with him, the jeep acting as the backdrop. This included an Australian, a New Zealander, one man from an Indian regiment, a Canadian, an Irishman, a man from a Scottish regiment, one from an English regiment and myself, representing the Welch Regiment, although truth to say I was English having been born in Chester, close to the border with Wales.

At the time we adopted various poses around the General, but the picture in the IWM was one in which he was not included, because it was used for a Commonwealth Christmas card after he had left the

Division. This card was the one my wife spotted and which now appears in this book. The two incidents which I have now described, namely meeting the Korean in Switzerland and seeing the photograph in the museum, have, as already stated, caused me to put pen to paper and record my own personal account of my experiences, feelings and opinions. For my part I was in the war from November 1951 until November 1952, and it was one of the longest and most unforgettable years of my life.

Although some of the names of my comrades of those days have faded, their faces and the incidents, situations, thoughts and feelings are still as clear as when they happened, but when I first put pen to paper, impressions, thoughts and feelings came tumbling down in endless line, one on top of another.

Was this really me all these years ago? Standing alone in the dead of night 12,000 miles from home, gazing out on a white, frozen, Siberian, windswept landscape, looking for an unseen enemy, rifle at the ready?

And who were these brave, gaunt-faced men trudging wearily past? What stories did they have to tell? Carried on a stretcher, shot in the ankle, one man sang as he went by.

As the shells rained down the bunkers shook and soil trickled down from the roof. Was our name on any of these bombs and shells?

But wait a minute, there must be a beginning to this story, and that beginning must surely be that day when I received my conscription papers to do my two years' National Service.

Let me now take the reader on a journey where laughter and sadness, pressure and relief, hope and despair live side by side and where fact is often stranger than fiction.

Chapter 2

Basic Training

Like many before me, and many after me, I was called up to do my two years' National Service on my twenty-first birthday, 5 January 1951.

Although I was a time-served engineer, I volunteered to join the infantry because I thought I would stand a better chance of becoming a physical training instructor, which seemed an interesting possibility. At the time I was a keen, fit athlete. Initially, I put my name down for the Royal Welch Fusiliers, because my father had been in that regiment during the First World War. In due course, I was sent a train pass and told to report to the army training camp at Brecon in mid Wales – wherever that was.

On the way down it was obvious the train was crammed with young men all heading in the same direction. Many were eighteen year olds, but if you were in a trade occupation you could defer your service until you were twenty-one, which is what I had done. On arrival we were herded into trucks and in no time at all were entering the gates at Brecon Army Training Centre, the HQ of the Welch Brigade, which was made up of the Royal Welch Fusiliers, the Welch Regiment and the South Wales Borders; whilst you were under initial training you could be allocated to any one of the three. Once you had completed your first six weeks you would be posted to the battalion in most need of new recruits. In my case I started in the Royal Welch Fusiliers, but at the end of my six weeks' training was posted to the Welch Regiment in Colchester. Little did I know at the time that the Welch Regiment had been earmarked for active service, and nothing could have prepared the new arrivals for what was about to happen in those first six weeks of initial training.

Once inside the camp gates it seemed that we had stepped into another world – maybe another planet. Army kit was dished out left, right and centre. We were given an army number which we were told we must never forget, because all our pay, kit and records were keyed to it. Incidentally, you never do forget – 22446936 Lance Corporal Williams.

Broken into groups of thirty-three, which we later realized was a platoon, we were then allocated to huts which were named after famous battles. Then, most importantly, we were allocated a bed and a locker, and ordered to blanco our kit for next day. 'When I say blanco your kit,' thundered the Corporal, 'I mean, all your kit. Now jump to it!'

Most of us were not over impressed by the Corporal's show of authority, but we set to blancoing our belts and webbing, plus putties, which seemed to be the only things which would take blanco. However, one poor lad was so nervous he started to blanco his shirt until the Corporal stopped him, but I could see the Corporal was quite pleased with the terrifying impact he had made on at least one recruit.

After being taken to the canteen for a meal we returned to our huts and were given a demonstration on how to put our kit on, make up our beds and arrange our lockers. We were then told it would be lights out at ten o'clock and reveille at six. This was no hardship for me because I had always been an early riser, but next morning, when the bugle sounded reveille and the hut door crashed open, I think some lads were more than a bit surprised, especially when the Sergeant rattled his stick ominously along the lockers and tipped a few of the lads out of their beds.

Having marched to breakfast and back the real job of turning civilians into soldiers began. 'You may have broken your mother's heart, but you won't break mine,' thundered the Sergeant as he pushed his face within an inch of a new recruit's nose. 'Don't look at me. Look to your front,' was his next pearl of wisdom, as he slowly made his way along the line of sprogs (army term for new recruits). We were a typical mixed bunch of lads as we stood there wondering what might happen next.

Although I was a 21-year-old time-served engineer, many of the lads were only eighteen and their occupations varied from shop assistants, to miners, market gardeners, office workers,and many other occupations, trades and even professions. It was a rich mix and a good training ground for life. Many of the lads were in poor physical condition and for some, those first six weeks were real torture. I was fortunate in that as a keen runner and footballer I was fit and so the physical training aspect of those early weeks was quite enjoyable.

As the Sergeant made his way further along each line he seemed to peer into the very heart of each recruit. His stock of cryptic sayings seemed endless and though they were often used in a personal way, they seemed to engulf the whole platoon or company when on parade. His rasping voice seemed to penetrate even the thickest skin.

As our training proceeded I realized that the techniques used were common to all sergeants and other non-commissioned officers (NCOs). It was all part of the conditioning techniques that changed civilians into fighting men. 'Hold your head up,' he would say, 'there's nothing in it!' 'Shoulders back, stomach in, chests out,' was another much-used saying. 'You're like loaves of bread marching about,' was another favourite he would use on new recruits trying to keep in step. These sayings would sometimes make you want to smile, but if the NCO in charge thought anyone found them even vaguely amusing he would follow them up with, 'Did I say something funny, soldier?' Then before the recruit could answer he would snap, 'Look to your front, don't look at me. I am not a pretty sight, am I?' Then once again before the recruit could answer, 'Don't answer that question, boy!' he would say. Then he would walk up and down the line staring in each individual's face. All clever stuff, designed to let you know that he, the NCO, or Corporal as was sometimes the case, was definitely in charge and you, the new recruit, were only making up the numbers.

Of all the sayings used, many of which must go back to the First World War and before, one of the most famous is the one that goes:

If you can move it – move it!
If you can't move it – paint it!
If it moves on its own – salute it!

The first six weeks was a constant round of marching, cleaning our kit, exercise, lectures and learning the basics of how to clean and fire our rifles and the Bren gun. We even had a Bren gun in the billet so that we could practise stripping it and putting it back together. From a standing position we were supposed to be able to dive down to the floor, put the magazine on the gun and get into the firing position within ten seconds. Quite naturally this led to a bit of betting when practised in the billet, which suited us and the Army. However, the lads didn't always show their true colours when carrying out this drill for the Corporal.

Most of the NCOs were decent blokes doing a professional job and very skilled and efficient they were. However, you always got the odd one who could best be described as a 'nut case'. Our resident 'nut case' had a face like chilled cast iron and an army rule book for a brain. Allied to this he had an unshakable belief that he was superior to the rest of the human race, one day this would be recognized and he would be raised to the exalted position of full corporal – a most unlikely possibility.

It wasn't so much his fanatical adherence to regimental standards that annoyed us, but his nasty habit of elevating his own ego by picking on the most timid member of the platoon. His method was to single out such an individual and make him demonstrate a particular skill whilst demeaning that individual in what, to us, was an unacceptable manner.

One poor lad from south Wales had worked in a shoe shop and had obviously led a sheltered life. Things physical and soldierly were not in his make-up. To make matters worse he had a rather large nose which easily turned red, so that he soon became known as Rudolf. Our fanatical soldier of the one stripe would pick on Rudolf at every opportunity, often using the time-honoured phrase, 'What are you, soldier?' He would then go right over the top and expect Rudolf to call himself stupid, or some other equally insulting phrase such as 'idiot'.

To a man we definitely did not prescribe to that formula, so whenever this particular lance corporal took us for any kind of drill we took it in turns to play him up. I remember him taking a lesson where he had to demonstrate how to dive down and load a Bren gun. Since we were all pretty expert by this time we all took turns in doing it, but each recruit would get it slightly wrong. Of course, our 'rule book' NCO couldn't see that it was a put-up job and he spent the afternoon demonstrating and re-demonstrating how it should be done, whilst we stood by enjoying the spectacle of him getting more and more wound up. By the end of the session he was convinced we were the thickest intake he had ever had. Ho ho!

As the days and weeks passed it was amazing how quickly everyone adjusted to army life and it wasn't long before we were marching, laying our kit out and behaving like men who had never known any other life. During this time many friendships were formed and a certain togetherness began to emerge.

I palled up with two lively characters, one from Holywell in north Wales – Jim Sibeon an ex-joiner, who sometimes gave his uncle a hand with his undertaking business. Jim was a tough, stocky lad with a great sense of humour. The other third of the trio was a lad called Jim (Ginger) Lamacraft who hailed from Abercunyn in south Wales. Jim was fiery like his red hair and although he had had a grammar school education, he had ended up working in a leather factory. Jim Sibeon always said that if Jim hadn't come down off the mountain for a drink, the Army would never have got him. The three of us became firm friends for the whole of our National Service and always went about together when off duty.

As with any group of people thrown together there was bound to be a few oddities. 'Morgan the sleep' was one. A nice lad but he had an unfailing ability to sleep anywhere at any time – 'on a clothes line', as they say. He could snore like a saw going through a rusty bucket and whenever we had a few spare minutes, where would Morgan be? You're right – fast asleep on his bed. Of course, people would sometimes tip him out of his bed which he seemed to take in good part, but at other times one or two mischievous types would get a fire bucket and plunge his hand in the cold water. Guess what happened – if the sleeper hadn't got a nappy on then something got wet. How did someone discover that bit of mischief?

During those early days quite a few nicknames were dished out and some were, to say the least, a bit harsh. Having said that, they usually had more than a grain of truth in them and 'Monkey Smith' was such a case. A short, stocky figure, he had a very primeval look about him and an unfailing ability to get things wrong. If anybody ever had two left feet it must have been Smith. No matter what the training was, whether it was presenting arms, marching or firing a rifle, Smithy could be relied on to do his own version of whatever was required. Most of the lads found this amusing, but when he received a food parcel and decided to eat it in the dark after lights out without sharing a crumb, well, that was something different.

Everyone received food parcels from home from time to time and the unwritten law when this happened was to share it round. Smithy's action was well noted and it was decided that this sort of conduct was not what was expected from an officer and a gentleman, as they say. The next time he received a parcel the lads laid a suitable trap for him. Some twenty seconds after lights out a designated member of the snatch squad grabbed his cake and in no time at all it was being handed round in the dark, each lad in the billet having a nibble. Poor old Smithy.

Later in the year when we had joined the battalion and were involved in some very serious battle training, Smithy committed the ultimate sin of firing his rifle at just about the worst possible moment he could have picked. Jim Sibeon, Ginger Lamacraft, Corporal Smith (no relation) and I had been out nearly all night lying in the cold on a listening patrol. We had crept up to the enemy positions and after several hours of crawling and listening, we had gauged the enemy's strength and layout of their positions. Based on this information our company lay blacked up, silent and patiently waiting for dawn, so that we could attack. Five minutes before 'kick-off', who let off a blank cartridge? Who was to make our lying in the freezing cold a waste of time? No prizes for guessing. Our one and only, never-gets-it-right, Smithy. Corporal Smith, our very experienced training Corporal, nearly exploded. 'Bloody hell,' he postulated as the round went off, 'that guy's two jumps ahead of a monkey.'

During the early part of our training everyone became fitter, stronger and more versed in the ways of the Army. Our rifles became like a third arm and you quickly became aware that if there was one piece of equipment which had to be given priority, it was the rifle. Cleaning and pulling it through became a daily chore, but when you were told to port arms for inspection, you soon realized that if you wished to avoid extra duties then a clean, shining rifle was essential. Anyone found deficient in this area of training was likely to end up at the cookhouse, scrubbing mountains of dirty pans or peeling equally mountainous piles of potatoes (spud bashing).

When a corporal or sergeant inspected rifles, they would come out with the usual crop of sarcastic sayings. 'If a spider crawled down my rifle barrel,' the NCO would say, 'it would come out blind. If it crawled down yours, laddie, it would drown in dirt and oil.'

Using the old .303 Enfield rifle, the British Army was famous for being able to fire fifteen rounds per minute, which in those days was considerable. In the First World War my father had told me that the Germans had often been fooled into thinking the British had more troops in a position than they had because of this ability to create rapid fire.

The Enfield rifle could also be used as a means of punishment for trainees if they were not making the effort required of them. The unlucky private who was given this type of punishment would be told to put his rifle above his head and double round the parade ground, until it seemed he was putting his back into it. There was also the practice of 'Pokey Drill' which was used to strengthen the hands and arms. This torture consisted of carrying out a whole series of exercises where the rifle was held at arm's length and manipulated to commands from the NCO. For young squaddies, who were not used to physical exercise, 'Pokey Drill' was absolute murder, but like most army training methods it was effective.

There is no doubt that the British Army had few equals in its methods of conditioning young soldiers for active service. Quite often they used group pressure to achieve their aims, and I vividly remember seeing one platoon marched to the cookhouse for dinner before being about turned and marched away because one member of the platoon was playing up. Thirty-odd young men all hungry and in sight of a well-earned meal, but then being denied it. The offending soldier in that group must have felt like running for cover.

Learning to shoulder and present arms was a skill which needed much practice, especially as we had to perform this task as one man. Nevertheless, it was not long before this challenge was being overcome, our efforts being spurred on by the frightening promise that anyone not making the grade would be back-squaded and would not get any leave at the end of the training. There is no doubt that when it comes to motivation the Army has a whole armoury of simple, direct methods and promises which engender the phrase 'If you can't beat 'em – join 'em!'

As part of our training we were given psychological as well as physical tests and, added to this, we were also given talks on hygiene and moral welfare. The films on what can happen if you catch VD were particularly impressive. The close-ups of what can happen to a penis when gonorrhoea or syphilis takes over was enough to put anyone off their dinner, as they say. Looking back, I don't think it would do the present generation any harm to receive such education. Promiscuity comes at a price.

And while on the subject of hygiene, it is worth relating an early experience I had which I am sure would not happen in this day and age. Early one morning I was detailed to report to the wash-house and when I got there I was surprised to find a Private N sitting in a bath with a corporal standing over him. My job was to give this lad a good scrubbing – and I do mean scrubbing. I felt sorry for him, but what had to be done had to be done. Private N took it all in good part, even managing to crack the odd joke. Later we became good friends and I learned that he had come from a large, poor family where personal hygiene was not a big factor. Once again, the Army's simple, direct answer to a problem had worked, though I suspect many modern psychologists would find reasons why other, more sensitive methods would be preferred.

To my surprise, after only three weeks, I was given a stripe, but was told I might lose it when I joined the Battalion, unless there was a vacancy.

One long-service regular soldier called Corporal Jones seemed quite miffed at the thought of me getting a stripe after such a short period of time. After all, he had been in the Army some sixteen years or so to get his two stripes. He worked in the armoury, but on the odd occasions when we met he would do his best to irritate me. Having worked in engineering, which was a good school for learning how to take a joke, I was impervious to his remarks. On one occasion he passed a remarked to the effect that to give useless National Servicemen a stripe was a waste of time, to which I replied that if I couldn't do better than corporal after twenty years I would give up. Oh, did that upset him!

However, when some sixteen months later he arrived in Korea as a late newcomer to Hill 355, he was more than glad to show friendship to anyone who would speak to him. His niggling, bullying ways when in the Brecon training camp had won him few friends, but as a late arrival in Korea he was now the novice amongst seasoned veterans. I was mending some shelled-out telephone lines in B Company's area when I met him outside a bunker, and I could see straight away that he was a worried man. He was full of nervous questions. 'What is it like on patrol?' 'Do you get much shelling?' 'Where is the best place to have a bunker?' 'What are the lads like on patrol?'

My answer to all these questions was, if you treat the lads right, you will be OK. He knew what I meant by this remark, and when I had mended the telephone line I went to see my old mate Jim Sibeon, who was a B Company signaller. Jim laughed when I told him I had met Corporal Jones. 'He's a worried man,' said Jim, 'because he's detailed to go on his first patrol this week, and some of the lads have been joking to him that he might have enemies in front and behind him.'

The next time I saw Corporal Jones he was a changed man. Gone was the old arrogance, to be replaced with a much more acceptable style of leadership. Training and active service are two different things, as our camp-based NCO had found out, and there was no doubt the change in the balance of power was better for all concerned. Corporal Jones's taste of 'humble pie' had definitely done him good.

Have you ever seen a man fishing on the side of a parade ground? We could hardly believe our eyes when we first saw this strange sight, which turned out to be an old soldier trying to work his ticket, as they put it. Not an easy thing to do in those days. It must have worked eventually, but not before he had been given a hard time.

In 1951 the Second World War had only been ended six years, so as a long serving soldier he must have been in the Army at that time and I suspected that he had his own good reasons to want to get out. Whatever they were, the Army was not prepared to make life easy for him and we often saw him being doubled round the parade ground and slopping out blocked and dirty toilets. One of the corporals told me that they even had him woken in the night to carry out various duties, in order to try and break his determination. When I spoke to him in the canteen one day he seemed a reasonable sort of person, but he said that he had lost all interest in army life and was for out. More than that he wouldn't say. Shortly after this occasion he disappeared. The general opinion was that he had been discharged, but there was the outside chance he might have been sent to Colchester detention centre, which was a chilling thought. Any regulars you spoke to who had any experience of that unit always described it in such terms as, 'a hell-hole', 'the pits', 'the end of the line' – such was its reputation. Over the years I think the Army has had to modify its methods of punishing soldiers, but my father, who had been on the North-West Frontier in India, prior to the First World War, had witnessed men being pegged out on the ground, or tied to the wheel of an artillery gun, to burn and sweat in the midday sun. Harsh measures indeed.

Somewhere around the fourth week of our training we were taken by truck into the Welsh hills to a place called Cwyn Gwdy. Translated into English we were told it was Welsh for 'hell-hole'. As it turned out this was a very apt description. The place was hidden in the Brecon Beacons and used as a firing range. On the day we arrived it was blowing a howling snowstorm and our billet was a redundant Nissen hut with no lights and no beds – just straw mattresses. The evening meal was a small portion of stew so that by seven we were all hungry and not a little cheesed off with our 4-star accommodation.

There we were, all sitting in the dark with nothing to eat and nothing to do – that was until Jones 58 rushed into the hut loudly whispering, 'I have got it.' Got what? we all thought. Would you believe it our hero had stolen a couple of loaves of bread, from where we neither knew nor cared. At that moment I am sure no jury in the land would have convicted him – certainly we wouldn't have done. In no time at all we were all munching dried bread, enjoying it as if it was prime chicken.

What was happening to us? Who would have thought that in four weeks a group of young men, from all walks of life, could be plucked from their homes and jobs, planted in a spartan, dark hut, in the freezing cold, and made so hungry that they would eat stolen bread and, at the same time, class the man that stole it as a hero? The army system was beginning to work. Jonnah, as we called him, had a rare talent for scrounging and making the best of a bad job. When we eventually went to Korea he became a batman to an officer who told me he was the best batman he had ever had, but that he was never quite sure whether Jones was batting for him or he was batting for Jones. Thereby hangs a tale.

After a fitful night's sleep we were up early, washed and shaved in cold water, before assembling at the range to get some serious target practice in. The snow was still falling as we lined up ready to fire a few zeroing shots, before adjusting our rifle sights. Our first few shots were reasonable, but as the cold bit into our fingers so the firing began to deteriorate. Flags for misses began to appear from one end of the firing butts to the other. However, the weather and conditions we were experiencing now would seem mild in comparison to what we would experience in Korea where the temperatures can drop to a low of minus 45^0, at which point our boots would start to freeze to the ground if we stood still for four or five minutes. Nevertheless, it was in its own way a foretaste of things to come, but we couldn't know that at the time. Somehow or other we managed to get some rifle scores which were just about passable, so after three days we were trucked back to camp.

As the three trucks rolled up to the gates, we were met by the camp's 'Mad Major' (every camp had one). Scowling fiercely he demanded to know why the shooting scores were so low. No explanation seemed to satisfy him, so in no time at all we were back in the trucks heading once more towards that dismal rifle range. This did not go down well with the sergeants and other NCOs, especially so because they had been given a dressing down in front of us lads.

When you are on a firing range you take it in turns to fire at the targets, and then act as target movers and scorers in the butts. With a little unofficial coaching from our irate NCOs we soon learned the art of making a bullet hole in the target by the use of our 'pig sticker' bayonet. This discovery dramatically improved the scores which was good news for everyone, except our 'Mad Major', and we were soon once again rolling back into camp. Begrudgingly he accepted the new scores, though by the look on his face he didn't really believe them.

As we neared the end of our six weeks' training I could see a dramatic change taking place which was quite amazing. Instead of the disorganized rabble of five weeks earlier, we were now beginning to look and behave like soldiers. Our brasses shone like gold, our boots were so polished you could see your face in the toe caps, and on the parade ground we marched and drilled as one man.

It was at this time that we had to take a whole series of physical tests which were scored against a standard. This involved doing 'x' amount of gymnastics such as press-ups, bar chin-ups and running a mile against the clock, plus a final test which involved a cross-country run. The first part of this was up a steep hill so, being a keen runner, I set off up the hill at a fast pace, but on descending the other side I caught up with the race marshals, who were still pegging out the full course. They were very surprised because they had expected the steep hill climb would slow everyone to a walk. Although I enjoyed these physical activities and did not drop any points, for some lads who had never exercised before, they were a really gruelling test. Marching certain distances in a given time was also another feature of this final training phase.

It was at this time that we were asked to form platoon football teams for an inter-platoon competition. Behind the scenes there was some hefty betting as to who would win this competition. Quite naturally we thought it would be us but, to our surprise, we found out that our Company Sergeant Major was going to turn out against us in the final, no doubt hoping to protect his bet. It was said he had played for the battalion team so we knew we would have to keep an eye on him, and who better to do this than our very good full back, Ivor Davies.

Ivor had a score to settle with the Sergeant Major because for some reason, known only to himself, he had taken a dislike to Ivor and had never lost the chance to give him a hard time. Normally the Sergeant Major was a strict but fair soldier, except where Ivor was concerned.

On the day of the match the ground was wet and heavy, which suited Ivor and I. We soon established that we were the better team and I had the satisfaction of scoring the winning goal in a 1 – 2 victory, but Ivor's satisfaction was far greater than anyone else's. He, it was, who took it upon himself to mark the Sergeant Major and mark him he did. At every opportunity Ivor landed him in the mud, each time offering to hand him up. There was no such thing as yellow or red cards in those days, or Ivor would have got a full house. Strangely enough, I think this personal encounter caused the Sergeant Major to have a grudging respect, so that it was noticeable thereafter that he did not pick on Ivor as before. Sport is a great leveller and often causes opponents to have respect for each other, even though they may not like each other.

The action-packed first six weeks passed slowly in one sense and yet quickly in another. None of us had ever packed so much into such a short space of time, so it was with considerable excitement that we approached our final test, which was the passing-out parade. Once this was over we were told we could go on two and a half weeks' leave, prior to joining our battalion.

Only one recruit was put back for more training and that was poor old Rudolph. This kind, timid lad from the Valleys was one of those people who had no sense of timing. His normal walk was rather disjointed and when he tried to march he was frequently out of step. On the firing range I remember watching him close his eye as he pressed the trigger, which is not exactly the best way to hit the bull, and no matter how hard he tried on some of the physical exercises, he seemed doomed to get it wrong.

As Jim Sibeon and I walked across the parade ground to draw our train passes for leave, we got a glimpse of poor old Rudolph marching on his own at the side of a new intake. Jim and I could only guess how the poor lad must have felt, but we felt extremely sorry for him. Chased around, shouted at, made to feel insignificant and then the final ignominy of being put back for retraining without leave. It must have been the worst ordeal of his life. I often wondered later what eventually happened to him and whether National Service did him any good. It certainly made him face a reality he would never have volunteered for, and who knows, it might have helped him in later life, but only he would know that.

Chapter 3

Joining the Battalion

The leave we got before joining the Battalion was very acceptable and seemed quite generous. Industrial leave in those days only amounted to one week per year, plus statutory bank holidays, Christmas and a couple of days for Easter, so something like seventeen days was a real bonus.

Of course, National Service pay was only one pound ten shillings (£1.50p) per week, which was not comparable to the £5 to £6 per week I could have earned as a craftsman at that time. Later, when our battalion took over from the Australians in Korea, we were amazed to find out that they received one pound ten shillings per day! This was why so many men in the Australian Army turned out to be British citizens who had gone to Australia on the £10 immigration scheme. When they arrived 'down under' they had, in many cases, found that life out there was not exactly a bed of roses, and the only way to make their fare home reasonably quickly was to join the Aussie Army. 'All that glitters is not gold.'

When I returned home to Chester for my leave I found out that the first question everyone asked was, 'When are you going back?' People say it without thinking, but after a while you find it difficult not to laugh. My mother and father were more than pleased to welcome me home, but my ex-serviceman father was amazed to see I had already earned one stripe. Sadly my brother Jim, who was ten years older than I, was in a poor state of health as his kidneys were failing due to him having Type 1 diabetes. It had started when he was ten years old and although he took insulin everyday, treatments were not as advanced as they are today and kidney transplants were out of the question. Sadly, Jim was not expected to live the year out, although today he most certainly would have been saved. During the war he was very upset because he could not join the Army due to his illness, but as a young teenager at that time (nine when the Second Word War started and fifteen when it finished) I was glad of his company during the air raids.

Chester got its share of bombs due to the fact it was near Liverpool, and also because it had an airfield and was a barrack town.

When the air raids were on my mother and I would go to a local shelter to join people from round about. People would chat and sing to pass the time, but my brother would often call in and take me home with him. Strangely enough, I always felt secure with him, even when doors and windows shook with the blast from bombs. At this time my father worked for the Stork Margarine factory at Bromborough, so was working seven days a week to keep essential foods flowing. He was also an air-raid warden there and on one occasion he put out seventeen incendiary bombs in one night. He was very committed to the war effort because being a veteran he knew what was at stake.

My leave passed all too quickly and I was soon back in camp bulling up my kit as I waited to join the Welch Regiment at Colchester. By now we had learned a few tricks of the trade such as putting sixpenny pieces in the oil bottle hole in the butt of our rifles. When we gave a butt salute to an officer, we were required to slap the butt of our rifle whilst at the slope, and would get an impressive 'click'. The illusion was that our hand had caused this click, which was just not possible. When we had first joined up, the drill NCOs pretended that this result could be gained by the vigour with which we executed this particular drill. Until we found out about the particular trick, we nearly bust our hands trying to do the impossible. Another curiosity, which seemed impossible to achieve until we discovered how to do it, was that of getting your trousers to hang nearly over your putties. It was solved when we found out that our Corporal had a string of small lead weights on the inside of his trousers so that they neatly circled his gaiters. All clever stuff!

We were informed that prior to leaving camp we were to have a brigadier's inspection. A likely story! However, on this occasion it was true. No one, but no one in their wildest dreams could have believed what a comedy our 'Monkey Smith' would turn this serious occasion into. The drill was that the Brigadier would be accompanied by the RSM who would, on entering the room, call us all to attention. In due course the door opened and the command, 'Room 'shun!' was given. So far so good. As the Brigadier and RSM walked up and down, if they stopped at a particular bed to inspect the kit, that soldier whose kit it was would 'about face', to face his kit, then, when the inspection was complete, 'about face' again. Last in line was our 'never-get-it-right Smith', and what did he do? His 'about face' was done all right, but as the Brigadier made to leave, the RSM gave the command, 'Stand at ease!' In typical army fashion, the RSM had said during rehearsal, 'When you stand at ease, lift your foot up six inches and stamp it in twelve.' In other words, make it really vigorous. Make the billet boards shake.

What did Smith do? He lifted his foot high in the air and stamped it in a fire bucket which was next to him. Charlie Chaplin couldn't have done better. Such an incident would make a cat laugh, as they say. Even the Brigadier and RSM were not impervious to this almost impossible feat, and I could see that as they left the room they were, like us, ready to burst with laughter. I often wondered whether Smithy was really that daft, or whether it was a one-man protest against a life he had been thrust into without his consent.

Before leaving Brecon Camp I had a score to settle with our resident borrowing Corporal. I was, when I first arrived, daft enough to loan him £2 which was more than my army pay for a week. The first time I asked for it back he made some lame excuse, but when I mentioned it to our hut Corporal he said, 'You'll be lucky to get it back!' I then found out he had borrowed from a number of people and that he worked this scam with every new intake. He was a big, bluff man who when put under pressure to pay money back would adopt a menacing attitude. He was, in simple terms, a bully. If there was one thing I couldn't stand, it was a bully, so when I went to see him for the final time it was a case of, I get my money or we mix it.

When I confronted him he tried raising his voice and asked me what I was going to do. I adopted an equally menacing attitude and told him. I could see him momentarily deflate and as I moved towards him he threw my £2 on the bed and muttered something to the effect I would have to watch it. I knew I had outgunned him because had we fought we would have been put on CO's orders which would not be good for either of us, but for him being a corporal, and a regular soldier, it would have looked doubly bad. Borrowing off new recruits could have cost him his stripes and spoilt some of his other scams. Also, like most bullies, he was a coward at heart. When I told our hut Corporal about the incident he was mighty pleased, because he was a decent bloke and when he told me I was the first one to get my money back I was more than happy.

One of the landmarks in National Service was the regular queuing up which had to be endured. Queuing for breakfast, queuing for dinner and tea – queuing for every bit of army kit. However, the most unpopular queue of all was lining up for your inoculations. By the time I finished my army service I had had over twenty inoculations and vaccinations recorded in my pay book. I was never a big believer in inoculations and whether they did me any good I will never know, but I do know some of the lads dreaded them. One Welsh lad called Griffiths had a hole in his arm the size of a sixpence as a result of the needle but he did not complain for fear of being back-squadded and losing his leave. Other lads had considerable pain and ran a temperature, but in those days it was a case of 'soldier on'. I think it is true to say that in some cases the same needle was used for a large number of people. Wiped with surgical spirit it was a case of, 'Next please!' If you were at the end of the queue, hard luck.

Of course we didn't envy the medical officer who carried out these medical exercises and we often used to laugh about some of the inspections they had to do. How many people would fancy the job of looking at 800 backsides for piles, or inspecting an equal number of penises for VD or similar? The lads used to make lots of jokes about this side of army life. Wife: 'Hello dear, have you had a hard day? I have got your favourite dinner. Sausages and liver.'

There were also similar jokes about people trying to fail their medicals to avoid National Service, for example:

Medical doctor: 'I see that you have had yourself castrated young man.'

Young man: 'It was an accident sir.'

Medical doctor: 'Well, you have failed your medical lad because you've got flat feet.'

The Army, quite rightly in my opinion, is based on tradition, much of which is related to morale and active-service conditions. Even the jokes which bounce around are often passed down from generation to generation. They may appear in various guises, but they are all part of the conditioning process called battle training. When things get tough someone would say: 'Dear Mum, please sell the pig and buy me out,' and back would come the reply, 'Dear Son, have already sold the pig. Soldier on.' In other words, once you're in there's no way out.

When lads first joined up the battalion barber would say to new recruits, 'How do you want your hair cut, laddie?'

Back would come the reply, 'Oh, just a nice trim, please.'

Then with one deft movement the barber would go straight up and over to leave the helpless victim like a shorn sheep. No hard feelings, of course, it was just the army way of doing things, but on active service short hair is less likely to get infected by lice.

The sequel to the first round of haircuts would be an inspection parade at which the NCO would stand right behind one hapless recruit's left ear and bellow, 'Am I hurting you, young man?'

'No sir,' would be the reply.

Then would come a double whammy for the new recruit. 'Then I bloody well should be!' thundered the NCO. 'I am standing on your hair – get it cut!' And then he would finish off with, 'What is my rank, soldier?'

The now nervous recruit would say, 'Sergeant – or Corporal – sir,' whichever it was. The NCO would then bellow even louder, 'I am not a sir. What am I?'

By now, more often than not, the soldier in question would be utterly confused, which was all part of the breaking down process. The NCO would then tell the victim to fall out and go back to the barber. He didn't really need another haircut but the barber knew the drill and would go over his head once again. All good clean fun, if you like that sort of thing. Of course, the effect of this charade on the other recruits would be to make them wonder what you had to do to please the NCO in charge. The answer, of course, was always to try harder. The result of this was that if anyone got even a small amount of praise it was like pure gold.

'A good soldier never looks behind' was another saying which embodies the spirit of forwards and upwards, and it is this 'never say die spirit' which makes the British Army such a formidable foe. My father told me one story from his wartime experiences which clearly shows this attitude and spirit. Wounded on three separate occasions he was, after returning from convalescence, posted to a forward company who were taking over from the French. In conversation with one of the Frenchmen he was told that this part of the line was very quiet. They had not had any action for a couple of months, which was not the British way. The day my father's regiment moved in, he was detailed for a patrol into enemy territory. That night, they blacked up and went out to probe the enemy. Father said that within an hour all hell was let loose and he had to spend two days in a shell hole before he could get back to his own position, so great was the barrage of German gunfire.

The British had arrived!

Chapter 4

Battle Training in Earnest

If anyone thought that the first six weeks was tough then compared to the next eight months it was a picnic. From the moment we arrived at Colchester Barracks to join the Welch Regiment we were subjected to non-stop battle training. Within the first five or six weeks we had fired practically every weapon known to the British Army at that time. Rifle, light machine-gun, Sten gun, 2-inch mortars, hand grenades, and what was probably the crudest and most diabolical weapon used by the British Army, namely the PIAT.

The PIAT had been hurriedly developed during the war to be used as a hand-held anti-tank weapon, but it could best be described as a drainpipe which fired anti-tank bombs. To load the monster you had to sit on the floor with the gun between your legs, with feet resting on two knobs halfway down the barrel. You then pulled back on the stock of the gun to load it. The spring was exceptionally strong, so that unless you really put your back into it, you would be snatched forward.

The first time this procedure was demonstrated by our very experienced corporals, Smith and Blowing, it was carried out sitting on a table. Of course, when the lads tried out this tricky method of loading the PIAT, about half of them landed on the floor, with the PIAT on top of them. When it came to the actual firing, that was another matter altogether. The first time out on the range Lamacraft and I agreed to be first to have a go with the PIAT loaded up with a live bomb. To fire the missile we had to get into a slit trench and while I leaned into the gun, Lamacraft grasped my right shoulder and leaned into me to support my shoulder against the recoil, which was enough to knock your shoulder out. Our practice shot was at a blanket which was stretched out some 50 to 80yds away, but we soon found out that you were lucky if you could hit the side of a house with this monstrosity. When it actually fired it was like standing next to a 25-pounder with your ear on the barrel. It left your head 'singing' for hours afterwards.

The last twenty years of my working life was spent as a full-time safety officer working in large companies and I now realize that some of my hearing loss could well be attributed to this weapon, and the time I later spent in Korea with 3-inch mortars.

Whilst on schemes and marches we were made to carry this unpopular piece of equipment, each member of each section taking it in turn to shoulder the PIAT. As can be imagined, no one wanted to hold on to it for even a few minutes longer than was absolutely necessary, especially when marching loaded up with full kit. The ironic thing about this cleverly designed torture was that in actual fact this particular piece of armament was obsolete and, as far as I know, never used in warfare after 1946. The bazooka which replaced it was a far superior weapon and much easier to fire. Another weapon which we used at that time was the Energa grenade, which was fired from a rifle which had an adapter fitted. To despatch this rather crude bomb you had to put your arm through the rifle sling in a manner which allowed you to hold the rifle against your body. To actually fire it, you had to 'snatch' the trigger in order to prevent injury to the finger. The bomb usually went anywhere rather than where it was specifically aimed, which meant that under war conditions you would have to get very close to a tank in order to hit it, and the odds would be that you might end up as a casualty as well.

During this part of our training the firing range became our second home and while some of the firing was a bit boring, there were times when it got exciting. Priming and throwing grenades was such an occasion. The training grenades had something like a ten- to twelve-second fuse so that after a grenade was thrown you had to watch it land, count three or four, then duck down behind the sandbag bay as it went off. The really exciting bit was when it didn't go off. When this happened, the person whose grenade it was had to go out with the Sergeant and sandbag the offending grenade, which was then blown up with gun cotton. Looking back, I can't help wondering whether some of the grenades were primed with dud fuses. The instructors had a way of making most things a bit larger than life. Whatever the reality was there's no doubt that the possibility of having to sandbag an unexploded grenade heightened everyone's awareness of the need to prime the grenades properly.

Another branch of our training which tested our skill and determination was the 500yds firing range run-down. This involved firing your rifle at the target from a range of 500yds and then running

100yds to the 400yds point to do the same, so that eventually you ended up on the 100yds point, from where you fixed bayonets and charged. It is easy to appreciate that on a windy day you would have to fire half the width of the target to one side to allow for your bullet being blown off course so there were plenty of white flags for misses at 500yds. On one occasion the RSM turned up and was soon heard to bellow, 'This is more like the Festival of Britain, than a firing range. Sort it out, Corporal!' Gradually our skills with small arms became more and more acceptable so that by the summer we had all qualified for our marksman's pay, which added a few shillings to our basic pay.

After our first few weeks in barracks we were shipped out to the wilds of East Wretham in Norfolk. The area and the weather were very bleak and the sheepskin liberty bodices we were issued with were very welcome. We were bedded down in old Nissen huts which were a leftover from the Second World War. They were spartan, as usual, but we soon made ourselves comfortable. Cold water was the order of the day for washing in, but by now we were getting used to the army way of doing things.

In this part of Norfolk there was a huge battle training area which was commandeered during the Second World War. Within this area whole villages, farms and even a church had been taken over in order to allow very realistic training: house-to-house clearing and combat, a lot of patrol work, endless route marches. There must have been a lot of heart searching in Parliament when the area was first evacuated, as with other counties in the UK similarly affected.

Norfolk being a very flat county, and as the crow flies not that far from Scandinavia and Russia, it was subject to biting winds and freezing night temperatures. We soon came to appreciate the old saying, 'Lazy winds, they didn't go round you, they went straight through you'. This was especially true when you were lying in the heather at two o'clock in the morning watching the frost settle around you, as you strained to hear snippets of information from the 'enemy'.

Jim Sibeon, Lamacraft, Private Newall, Corporal Smith and myself became quite expert at this type of work. Perfectly camouflaged with old rags and coloured bunting, it was amazing how close we could get to other defending battalions. Hands and faces blacked up, we could literally disappear in the darkness. On one occasion we were out on patrol and when we heard someone coming we just squatted down motionless. It turned out to be an enemy patrol, but so invisible were we, they passed within inches of us without realizing we were there. That is, all except the last man who must have glanced down and seen the whites of Jim Sibeon's eyes. The shock made him jump sideways, but he hurried away into the darkness without a word. What he really felt and thought we never found out.

During these months of battle training we developed a good relationship with our training Corporals, Smith and Blowing. Both had seen service in the Middle East and were very experienced in weapon and battle training. They were strict but fair, with a roguish element in their make-up which no doubt would prove useful in difficult situations. They were great borrowers if they could get away with it – they rarely bought toothpaste, shoe polish and blanco. Their style was very smooth and they would always use friendly banter before getting the killer punch in. 'You did all right there today, Johnson. Oh, just lend us your shoe brush and polish a minute.' Goodbye shoe polish and brush. A favourite trick of theirs at dinner time was to sit either side of one of the lads who was still a bit fussy about his food. If the sweet was something they liked they would start a conversation about something not exactly dinner-time conversation. Smithy (Smudger) would say, 'Did you see that bloke in A Company being sick yesterday?' Then he would go into graphic detail, such that quite often the victim would push his food away. 'What a shame to waste good food,' Blowing would say. Then the pair of them would tuck into this windfall and the last thing the victim would hear as he left the table was Smith and Blowing thanking him for his generosity.

When carrying out inspections these two could spot the slightest defect in turnout or performance. However, it was a fact that Jim Lamacraft was so immaculately turned out each day that he was hardly, if ever, caught out on morning parade. This had not gone unnoticed by Messrs Blowing & Smith, so in typical army style they decided that on a particular morning they would show the platoon that even Lamacraft was not faultless. As they moved along the line they did their usual, 'Tighten your belt, soldier.' 'Get your cap badge shined, soldier.' 'Head up, lad,' and all the usual minor prods, but when they came to Jim they began to inspect him from head to toe. Haircut OK, cap badge glistening, uniform pressed OK. It really began to look as if Jim had beaten the system and he couldn't help showing the flicker of a smirk.

All of a sudden, Corporal Blowing bellowed, 'Lift your boot, Private Lamacraft.'

Jim slowly bent his knee to show the sole of his boot.

'Look at this,' yelled Corporal Smith as he inspected the sole of his boot. What had he found? 'Only thirteen studs, not sixteen as required,' said Corporal Smith with an air of triumph.

'Report to the canteen at 1800 hours for fatigues,' announced Blowing. Once again the system had triumphed, but even Jim appreciated the joke.

Our day-to-day contact with our training NCO was bringing us all closer together as a team. One could almost say 'a family'. Fatigues weren't too bad, really, because at the end of the mountainous spud-bashing, Dixie-cleaning, floor-polishing work you usually got a slap-up meal from the leftover food from teatime.

This early training, which was applied so vigorously, would hold the lads in good stead when they eventually landed in Korea. Badly trained or untrained troops are much more vulnerable in active-service conditions, and my father told me of one case that he personally knew about when a young officer arrived at the front after only a short training period. This would be in about 1916 and because of his lack of experience and discipline he thought he could bob his head up to see if he could spot the enemy. My father tried to advise him against this, but within seconds the officer was shot through the head by a sniper. On active service second chances are not always an option.

Whilst the Army won most of the encounters with regard to discipline and training, there were occasions when individuals and groups won the day. As part of your survival kit, as a group of National Servicemen in an infantry battalion in those far-off days, it was essential to have someone in the platoon or company who could be relied on to find out what was likely to happen next, before it actually happened. In other words, a 'wide boy'. Ours was Jones 58 (Jonnah). This was the same Jonnah who managed to steal a loaf of bread when we were nearly freezing to death on the firing ranges up in the wilds of the Brecon mountains. Yet, smart as he was, when it came to finding out such things as how to get back into camp after lights out, he was not noted for being the smartest soldier on parade. On one occasion I remember him getting ready for morning parade when, after a night out, he looked an absolute mess. Brasses dull, uniform creased, and boots nowhere near parade standard. I said to him, 'Are you trying to commit hari-kari or something?' But to my surprise he only grinned and said, 'I'm going to stand next to you and there won't be a problem.'

Being fairly tall I was always used as a 'right marker' on parade which meant that I was first to get in line and everyone lined up on me. To stand next to me seemed to be the worst place he could have picked, but when he undid his top tunic button and tapped his nose in the way that roguish people sometimes do, I realized what his risky plan was. As part of army procedure in those days, if a soldier had a button on his tunic not fastened he was told to take one step backwards and do up the offending button. Jonnah's philosophy was that by standing next to me on parade, the Sergeant taking the inspection would spot his undone button before he reached us and would then give the command. 'One step back, soldier, and fasten that button.' And so it was. Jonnah deliberately took his time fastening his button so that by the time he had stepped back in line the Sergeant has passed on and missed the other unsoldierly bits of our crafty wide boy. As the Sergeant passed down the line Jones 58 glanced up at me with a cheeky grin which said more clearly than words could convey, one up for me.

Whilst it was hard to beat the army system you could on occasions use it against itself. Such a situation arose when one bright sunny morning I found myself late for parade. I had been serving mother nature and when I returned to the barrack room everyone had left and was on parade. To have slunk on parade as a late starter would have been a sure way to get myself put on fatigues. So I shouldered my rifle, marched smartly on parade and came to a halt in front of the Company Commander. I then gave him a smart butt salute with my rifle, making the sixpenny bits in the butt rattle as if I had nearly broken the butt. Then in my best imitation of an RSM I bellowed, 'Permission to fall in, sir!'

'Permission granted,' came the reply and I marched straight into my usual position, which made everyone realign to let me in. So there I was home and dry and not a question asked.

Later on the Sergeant said to me, 'That was a chancy one, Williams,' to which I had to nod in agreement, but really the Sergeant didn't have a problem with someone who did it the army way. You don't really beat the army system, you join it!

Whilst stationed up in the wilds of the army battle training area of East Wretham, we would sometimes get a Saturday in Thetford, or very occasionally Norwich. Thetford was only a small town, but Norwich was a fine old Roman city very similar to my home town of Chester. Our trips there, though infrequent, were very much appreciated, especially after our many three- and five-day training schemes. These small but welcome breaks from our intensive training were the limit of our civilian contact, so imagine my surprise when I was summoned to the Adjutant's office, given a weekend pass and told I was going on leave to play football in the West Cheshire Cup Final. Before reporting for my National Service I had played for the Stork Margarine factory in the West Cheshire League and had helped them reach the final of this cup, but once in the Army I had given up all hope of playing in the final game itself. It had never crossed my mind that the club would write to our CO requesting my temporary release. Of course Lever Brothers, who owned the factory, were a very big and influential company, so no doubt a letter from them signed by the appropriate person had made this situation possible. Not only was I given a pass, but I was also given my train ticket and driven by jeep to Bury St Edmunds to catch a train. All of this was unusually generous for the Army so I guess someone must have written a very persuasive letter.

Eventually, I arrived home in the early hours of Saturday morning and after a brief nap caught a bus and then a taxi to the Port Sunlight oval ground where the final was to be held. I did not have the football chairman's number which meant I couldn't let them know I was on my way, and when I arrived they had almost given up hope of me playing. Since I had scored some thirty-five goals for the team before joining up they were as anxious for me to play as indeed I was. The player who was twelfth man selflessly and willingly stood down, and I was able to replay his generosity by scoring the winning goal in our 2–1 win. I still have the plaque which each of us received and, of course, our twelfth man also received his. With the match over I was soon on my way back to East Wretham and battle training once more.

In my early schooldays and early teens, I had lived for football, and was playing in the Senior Chester & District League at fifteen years of age. As a half back or centre forward I could more than hold my own, and by the time I was seventeen I was playing in the Welsh League for Connah's Quay and had attracted one of Chelsea's senior scouts. I signed amateur forms for them and arrangements were being made for my engineering indentures to be transferred to a London firm so that I could sign as a professional for that great club. Ted Drake was the manager at that time, having finished his playing career with Arsenal and England. I had been watched by the Chelsea scout for some six months before they signed me up, but I did not know this at the time. Unfortunately, just before I was due to go down there Ted Drake left the club and I received a letter telling me to wait. In the meantime a Mr Ted Davidson had taken over, but it was to be six months before I received another letter asking me to go to London. As it happened, I had received a nasty ankle injury at that time and felt so let down I decided not to go.

As a young player I was also fortunate to get some coaching from Tommy Jones, the Old Everton and Wales centre half. In his spare time Tommy had taken a Connah's Quay under-nineteen side under his wing, coaching them to such a high standard that they demolished all local opposition, and in 1948 got to the final of the under-nineteen Welsh Junior Cup. I worked with a number of the players and was persuaded to play for them, which gave me the opportunity to get many valuable tips from this master of playing and tactics. Several of the players got Welsh Junior International caps and we went on to win the Welsh Junior Cup, after a hard-fought game against Cardiff City under-nineteen side. The final at Aberystwyth was an exciting game which we eventually won 1–0. It was the first time for over twenty years that a north Wales side had won this trophy, but there was no doubt that the coaching of Tommy Jones was a major factor. When we got back to Connah's Quay the whole town turned out to greet us.

Few people will remember players like Tommy Jones now, because they would have to be in their seventies to do so, but not only was he a world-class centre half, he was one of the first players to leave a first division side to join a non-league club, whilst he was still at the height of his playing career. This was a shrewd move on his part because the maximum wage for footballers at that time was £10 plus £2 for a win and a £1 for a draw. As a player-manager with the Welsh League club Pwllheli, and manager of the local hotel/pub, he could easily eclipse that amount several times over. His great tactical and playing ability ensured that the club won many trophies.

After my demob I played for Pwllheli for a season, and it was at that time I was invited to Manchester United for a week's trial, during the closed season. At that time Manchester United had some very talented players. Duncan Edwards, Tommy Taylor and Bobby Charlton were all there, though Bobby Charlton was only about sixteen at the time.

During the closed season I used to run with Wirral Harriers which kept me fit, so that when I arrived at Manchester I was curious to find out just how fit the full-time professionals were. To my surprise I found I was equally as fit as any of them, even fitter than some. During the week that I was there I stayed at the large house where all the single players lived and enjoyed their company. They were all very enthusiastic and friendly, especially Duncan Edwards. Although younger than me, Duncan had enormous talent and was never happier than when he was kicking a football. I could easily see why he was so highly rated.

The atmosphere at United was very good but there was no doubt who was the boss. Everyone from the ground staff to the playing staff showed great respect for Sir Matt Busby. I had gone to United as a centre forward which is where I usually played, but in spite of the fact that I scored many goals in that position, my best position was really centre half. By the end of the week Sir Matt and Jimmy Murphy had realized this and in the last couple of trial matches they played me in that position.

When the week's trial came to a close I was called into the office and Sir Matt and Jimmy Murphy gave me an honest assessment of my playing abilities. They said I was fit enough and strong enough to meet United's standards and that I was a very good tackler and user of the ball. Most importantly in their book, I wasn't afraid to meet a challenge, but because of my age (I was then twenty-three) they were not sure whether I would adapt to the United way of doing things. They were prepared to offer me a short-term contract to play in the reserves whilst they made their minds up, but on reflection I decided not to accept the offer. As an engineer in those days I could earn what they would have offered, plus half as much again playing in non-league football. I was also studying three nights a week at night school in order to pass an engineering National Certificate examination, so taking everything into account I was sure my decision was the right one. Matt Busby said that if I had joined the club when I was in my teens he was sure they could have used me to good advantage, but at twenty-three years of age they would need at least six months to be sure I could adapt.

When it comes to wages what a difference it is today. Some players are so highly paid they can earn what some people take a lifetime to earn, in just a season. Good luck to them whilst it lasts!

If I had joined United would I have been on that fateful flight when it crashed? What a terrible tragedy that was, what a waste of so many talented young men.

In the week I was at United I was very impressed with their coaching standards and Bobby Charlton would be the first to admit that much of his success was due to the efforts of Bert Whalley and Jimmy Murphy. It was Bert Whalley who arranged my trial and what a gentleman he was. Sadly he also died in the crash which was a great loss to all who knew him.

After United I played non-league football for another couple of years before a knee injury forced me out of the game, but I still look back on those far-off days with great pleasure and enjoy watching great players.

Having played in a reasonably good class of football both with and against some excellent players, and having watched many famous players over the past sixty years, I have come to the conclusion that football is a great sport. At its best it brings into focus many of life's most important attributes, both physical and mental – agility of mind and body, speed, skill, teamwork and courage – and there is no doubt in my mind that in sport young people learn the importance of playing to rules and, most importantly, handling success and failure. The discipline learned in sport is also a valuable lesson, which applies to all walks of life.

Chapter 5

Final Preparation for Active Service

Back in the Norfolk training area, life was getting tougher by the day. We realized that our destination would eventually be Malaya or Korea but we never gave these possibilities much thought at the time because we were too busy taking in fresh information, as well as taking part in numerous exercises.

On one of our night marches we had to do 12 miles in three and a half hours carrying our full kit over rough, unknown terrain. It was an inky black night and one of our lads, Jones 58, collapsed as we neared the end of the march. As I passed him in the dark the Sergeant was shining a small light into his ashen face as he tried to bring him round. There was no doubt Jones was really 'out of it', as they say, and later on they discovered that he was night blind. This meant he was no longer classed as A1 and could not remain as an infantryman. The poor lad was really upset when they posted him away from his mates, Ishline Hughes and Pritchard. These three were mates before they had joined up, and on their first day had arrived at Brecon half drunk. The Sergeant Major had been highly impressed, especially when he found out that they had been sick in his personal toilet. This very auspicious start had put the three of them in the frame, even before serious training had begun, but if the truth was known it did to some degree impress the training staff at Brecon.

As friends they were like naughty lion cubs. Often when we were in barracks they would have an all-in wrestling match which was highly comical to watch. It would start with the three of them facing inwards. Then in would go Ishline to get a lock on Pritchard, but as soon as this happened Jones would jump on Ishline. While Ishline was half choking, Pritchard Jones would be trying to screw Ishline's head off. As soon as Ishline let go of Pritchard, Pritchard would jump up and get a lock on Jones. And so with groans, moans and bursts of laughter they would wrestle away for half an hour or so, before they would all fall apart exhausted, each claiming to have won this impossible match. Basically they were good soldiers but their tendency to push their luck with corporals and sergeants inevitably landed them with several sessions of 'jankers' which they treated as some kind of a joke. When a soldier was on 'jankers' they would have to do everything at the double, but they were fit lads and they didn't seem to mind this sort of punishment.

There were, of course, some lads who disliked the Army intensely and never missed a chance to bemoan their lot. Some of them would have done a bunk, but they knew they would be brought back and charged with desertion. One such lad who loathed the Army intensely was called Lemon, and he not only disliked the Army, but made it known that if we were posted to Korea he wouldn't be going. And so it was!

Shortly after we found out we were going to Korea, Lemon woke up one morning complaining that he couldn't get out of bed. His story was that he had woken from a nightmare during the night and had found himself hanging from the window sill of our second-storey barrack room, after which he had fallen to the ground before crawling back upstairs to stagger into his bed. A likely story by any standard since our barrack room was easily 20ft above ground level.

When the Sergeant pulled back his bed sheets he was found to have some marks on his legs, which seemed to support his story to some degree, but to drop 20ft without breaking a leg seemed most unlikely. Without hesitation, the Sergeant sent for the MO and by the time we returned from training Lemon was gone, his locker and belongings cleared, and it was as if he had never existed. I suspected that the Army realized he was not cut out to be a soldier, which would have made him a liability to his mates on active service. No doubt they would have found him a suitable occupation to complete his National Service, though I doubt whether he would have enjoyed it. Although everyone thought Lemon was acting up a bit, it was a fact that he was prone to nightmares and on one occasion woke up shouting that there were snakes on the bottom of his bed. So who knows what went on in his mind?

During our stay in Colchester I became very friendly with a Corporal Oram, a Physical Training Instructor (PTI). He had been a professional boxer at one time, and because of my interest in PT, he had from time to time let me help him with his classes. I enjoyed this part of my training, the idea being that I would end up as an instructor myself.

As part of our training we did a bit of boxing, and he taught me a great deal about throwing punches and keeping a good defence. When I first sparred with him he kept catching me with neat sharp blows to the chin, and this really puzzled me until he explained that as I threw a left I was letting my right hand move away from my chin. Like the good professional he was he did not take advantage of my inexperience, but gradually and patiently showed me how to use my feet correctly, throw various punches, and what to do in clinches to get an opponent off guard.

'Never get caught with your legs crossed,' he would say, 'because you cannot punch your weight unless you are well balanced. Never throw a punch unless you mean it. Sloppy punches allow your opponent to counterpunch. Punch from the shoulder,' he would suggest, 'and keep your wrist in line with your arm and knuckles.' Under his coaching I soon became proficient at the basic boxing skills and eventually I got to a standard whereby I could give him a good workout.

As a young lad I had wrestled with my cousin Frank Cassidy who was a professional wrestler, so I had no fear of body contact sports. In fact, I had even wrestled with some of his older professional friends who had allowed me to throw them about. They were great characters and I can still remember some of the holds they taught me to this day.

When you exchange leather with an opponent, you usually gain respect for each other – so it was with Corporal Oram and I, and we became firm friends. I would hardly have guessed at that time what a tragic adventure Korea would be for this likeable character, or that I would represent the Battalion at boxing.

Looking back on National Service I can now see quite clearly what a great education it was. People from all walks of life were thrown together under a disciplined regime which allowed everyone to find their own level. In this environment people could measure themselves against people they would not normally have met. Some lads found they had hidden reserves of strengths and abilities they would never have recognized, while for others it was a sobering experience to find they were nothing like as clever or tough as they thought they were. The army standards of smartness and personal hygiene had much to recommend them and would certainly benefit many modern youths.

As I have mentioned, I had formed a firm friendship with two characters called Jim Sibeon and Jim Lamacraft during my initial training, and later, when I was posted to D Company of the Welch Regiment. Off duty we usually went out together and, like me, Jim Sibeon enjoyed physical sports such as running and boxing, so we would often train together. Added to this we were all in the same platoon and the same section, and because we worked well together we were often chosen to demonstrate various infantry skills. By the use of coloured hessian sacking and bunting we could make ourselves virtually invisible, even in open countryside. With our faces blacked up and our camouflage on we would blend into bushes, heather or even trees or grass, and when other companies were brought out to spot us, they rarely could until we were told to stand up. Sometimes we were so close to the lookers they could hardly believe their eyes when we made ourselves visible.

However, there was one skill our whole platoon used to demonstrate, which looked easy but was very difficult and needed much practice. This particular skill was called the moving truck retreat. The idea was that while the whole platoon were laid out in what was a rearguard action, with rifles, Bren guns, and everyone carrying full kit, a 3-ton truck would drive by at about 4 or 5mph. On a command, each section in turn would jump up and race after the truck, which had its tailboard down. The first man aboard would turn around and then as each man leapt at the truck he would grasp their hand or arm and yank them aboard. Using this technique a whole platoon of thirty-three could board a truck in a few minutes. It is easy to imagine that one or two of the lads would bash their shins or bruise themselves during this manoeuvre. As the Battalion gradually built up to full strength we were called on to demonstrate this skill to several squads of new recruits.

On one occasion we had one group who made the mistake of laughing when one of the lads got dragged along before being yanked aboard. 'Oh dear!' 'How sad!' 'What a laugh!' For the next ten minutes we were treated to a comedy act which could have been straight out of a Charlie Chaplin film, or a Monty Python sketch. On a command the recruits took up their positions lying in the heather and then as the truck drove slowly past the Sergeant gave the order. 'Withdraw by section.'

What a pantomime! Bang – crash – Ow! Rifles hitting the backs of heads as they got in each other's way before trying to jump for the truck. There were bashed shins. Some lay flat on the road as they missed their footing whilst making a frantic leap, as the truck drove away only half full with stragglers chasing after it. I think their Sergeant called it a shambles, but there was no doubt the lads had learned a valuable lesson. The easy way is hard, but the hard way is bloody unbearable!

I don't suppose that group of recruits would ever forget their first running withdrawal practice, and they would be wary about making a mockery of it in the future.

*

During the months before we embarked for Korea our training intensified at a steady rate. Many hours were spent on the assault course behind the barracks and because it was so handy we often used to practise on it in our own time. After much practice we realized that the way to get round the course with the least difficulty was to go for it right from the start. The course involved crawling through a tunnel, swinging over a water jump, mounting a 10ft wall using your mates' rifles as steps before jumping for the top, and getting across barbed wire by taking it in turns to lie across it while your mates used you as a stepping stone. Finally, you had to mount and get over rope netting, before going hand over hand on a steel frame above a water pit. All good clean fun, one might say, but there was no doubt that those of us who did a bit of practising in our own time benefited from this when we had to do it as a drill in battledress.

Of course, our star turn Smithy, of cake and blank fame, didn't subscribe to this extra practice, so that when his turn came under semi-battle conditions he was able to treat us to a first-class comedy act. Being a short, stocky lad his uniform never seemed to fit him properly, and he had a habit of not fastening his belt tightly enough, so when he emerged from the crawling tunnel his trousers were already at half mast. Immediately, the Sergeant and Corporal in charge saw the possibility of a rare comedy act in Smithy's predicament, so quite naturally they urged him on, not giving him time to pull up his trousers or adjust his rifle which was nearly strangling him. The next ten minutes or so had us all doubled up with laughter as the poor lad half staggered and half fell into the water jump, and generally stumbled his way round the course, everyone urging him on. It must have been murder for Smithy and never in his wildest dreams could he have imagined himself performing such a task under such conditions.

Generally speaking most of the lads got on well, but in the confines of a barrack room, with some thirty men in it, there were bound to be times when tempers got frayed and individuals got on each other's nerves. Mixed in with us National Servicemen was a smattering of regulars and their experience could be quite useful at times, especially when problems occurred of which no one had experience. Such an occasion arose when our Corporal Roberts decided to go on a series of binge-drinking sessions, often returning late at night to make himself very objectionable by wanting to wake people up and talk. One of our regulars was a Private Davies who had been in the Parachute Regiment, but he had broken his ankle and was no longer fit enough for that outfit.

'I know the answer,' said our adviser. 'Take the light bulbs out before he comes in. They can be put back when he's gone to bed.' What a good idea!

The first night it worked quite well, because when our befuddled Corporal found the lights could not be switched on he went to bed, instead of boring anyone who would listen with stupid conversation.

However, on the second night our inebriated Corporal got a bit abusive and after staggering round the room, sat on the edge of the bed next to mine. I told him to shove off, which no doubt annoyed him, but instead of having a go at me he staggered down the room and challenged Davies to a fight. I suppose he had guessed that Davies had initiated the no-light policy. With his brain out of gear and his legs full of marbles, Corporal Roberts was in no state to fight anyone. The outcome of this fracas was very, very predictable and in no time at all our drunken friend was lying on the floor with a bloody nose. Silly man!

This incident would normally have caused our Private Davies to be a marked man, but ever the wise old trooper, he went on CO's orders and by dinner time he was packing his bags to join the battalion band. Apparently he was also a bandsman and on his interview with the CO he must have said the right things. I was sorry to see him go because he was a likeable and useful character.

Of course, not every regular fitted in with us National Servicemen and when we first arrived at Colchester Barracks there was one regular already ensconced there who was a very strange character indeed. He was the sort of person you only meet once in a lifetime. Classed as a 'bog waller' (toilet cleaner), he was nicknamed 'the Bear'. This was because he had a big square head and a very dour face. Initially when we arrived this unusual character tried to convince anyone who would listen that he was the fount of all knowledge, but it soon became obvious that he was more than a bit odd – 'all mouth and trouser' as they say. Oddly enough he could recite a bit of poetry, but his style and demeanour made you wonder what his background was. Once we had settled in 'the Bear' began to show his true colours, which was to use his tall stories to find out who he could bully. Of course, if you bared your teeth he would quietly back off.

In the next bed to mine was a quiet lad nicknamed 'Jimmy Crow'. He was of gypsy ancestry and had swarthy dark looks with dark hair. Jimmy was a tough little character who was always up before reveille, but on one particular occasion he was just getting dressed when 'the Bear' suddenly smacked him across the face for no obvious reason. Bullies I cannot stand! A few seconds after this incident happened I was chasing 'the Bear' out of the barrack room and down the stairs. As he disappeared I slung a fire bucket full of water after him. Although annoyed we all had a good laugh and didn't think much more about it.

However, when we returned from training, 'the Bear' was nowhere to be found. Eventually one of the lads came in and said that he was standing outside asking if he could come in. We all agreed he could, as long as he apologized to Jimmy. This he duly did, but shortly afterwards he was transferred elsewhere. Unlike civilian life the Army can always find a place for even the most odd or awkward people.

During the summer of 1951 we spent most of our time in the Norfolk training area near Thetford, but before we were shipped out for battle training we did quite a bit of training at Colchester Barracks, which also gave Jim Sibeon and I a chance to do some athletics training on the excellent cylinder track there. Both of us were picked to represent the Battalion in the Inter-Battalion Divisional Meeting, Jim in the 3-mile event and myself in the 4 x 100yds and 4 x 440yds. A number of the lads were prepared to help us train, so Jim and I used to give them a start, then we would use them as pacemakers. We also used to run in boots sometimes and I found this useful for getting off the mark quickly. Compared to modern training techniques it may seem quite crude, but I could run a 10.3 hundred and a 52-second quarter mile. Using spikes after wearing boots certainly gave me a lift.

Unless it has been experienced it is hard to explain the feeling you get when you feel fit and your feet fly over the ground. Now in my late seventies I can still remember those far-off days as if they were yesterday, but sadly my legs no longer respond to my commands any more and speed is no longer mine to command. A few T'ai-Chi exercises keep me moving, but only at a very leisurely gait.

At the end of our training sessions, when we returned to the barracks sweating profusely, we developed a rather comical way of showering down. To the rear of our barrack room was a semi-circular area with taps and basins which was mainly used for cleaning dirty kit. It had a stone floor and drainage gulleys so when we were ready we used to shout, 'Wash down, lads!' and like a shot out of a gun, several of the lads would rush into this area and hurl buckets of water at us from close range. It sometimes turned into a bit of a water fight, but it was very invigorating and saved us the trouble of going to the showers which were at the other end of the parade ground. Of course the fire buckets which were used had to be refilled when the water bath had finished.

The divisional sports meeting was a very hard-fought affair which lasted two days, and, thanks to some excellent performances from some of our star athletes, the Welch Regiment eventually came out tops. The most outstanding performance was undoubtedly that of Sergeant Hughes who was an expert javelin thrower. Having come sixth in the AAA Games, his throw of some 170ft sailed out some 50ft further than anyone else's. In fact, it made some of the others look as if they weren't trying.

I was in the teams for the 4 x 100yds and 4 x 440yds events, both of which we won. In the 4 x 440yds I had the particular satisfaction of pulling back some 20yds and then giving a 10yds lead to our final runner. I received a personal congratulation from Lieutenant Colonel Dean, our commanding officer, which was a rare event, and my mate Jim Sibeon finished in the first twelve in the 3 mile event, to gain some valuable points. Jim wasn't a runner as such but if there was one thing he did have was guts and, of course, a great sense of humour.

One of the surprise results of the day was the high jump which was won by one of our cooks. Initially we thought it was a fluke that he had even qualified for this event, until later we found out he was an experienced harrier. We all enjoyed the joke, though I don't think the opposition did. What hidden talent there was when National Servicemen got together.

After this interlude we headed for the Norfolk training area and some very realistic training. We didn't know what our final destination would be, but many of us were beginning to think Korea or Malaya were distinct possibilities. Our training included some tough assignments including living in the back of a truck for five days while the trucks covered half of southern England. We only stopped for a few hours here and there, during which we were expected to dig in, but no sooner were we dug in than we were off again. A phased withdrawal they called it.

Standing or half-sitting in a truck hours on end is not exactly an invigorating exercise, especially when the stops were sometimes hours apart. It was, therefore, not surprising that during this exercise many of the lads became expert at urinating out of the back of a 3-ton truck – not a pretty sight! But when nature calls and no one answers, necessity becomes the mother of invention. During this particular exercise there was one act of charity which cost very little, but had a dramatic effect.

By the third day of the exercise nearly all the smokers had run out of cigarettes, which was no big deal for those of us who were non-smokers, but for those who were hooked, it was, as they say, 'murder'. From time to time the 9-mile line of trucks would halt for various reasons, sometimes for a few minutes, sometimes for an hour or so, but on one such a stop in a small town the miracle occurred. Due to the lack of fags it was noticeable that the swear rate and general aggravation had increased enormously until one kind gentleman tossed a packet of twenty cigarettes into the back of our truck. I think he might well have been a veteran of the last war, but whatever his motivation for this kind act there was no doubt that at that very moment the sun shone and the world became a better place; bloody awful became bloody marvellous and in a few minutes agony became ecstasy. Of course, in those days cigarettes were not seen as coffin nails and in most of the war films many a dying hero was sent on his way with a puff of his mate's last fag. Such is life!

In the final weeks of training out in the wilds of Norfolk, the sessions of weapon firing, digging in and marching became even more difficult and exhausting, culminating in a three-day, 60-mile march from Norfolk to Colchester. Marching on roads, in full battledress, in boiling hot weather, is not everyone's idea of fun, but the only way anyone could drop out was by collapsing, and even then the 'blood wagon' would soon have them back on the road unless they were a hospital case. Every evening when we pitched bivouac tents, feet were inspected and a few plasters dished out to desperate cases. One of our lads called Teddy Egan had twenty-two blisters on his feet, but he stuck it out without complaint.

During this march a very curious circumstance occurred which had to be seen to be believed. Several times a day the regimental band would be instructed to play some marching songs, but whenever we passed a field of cows, the cows would come charging across to listen with great interest and they would follow the band until a fence or hedge prevented them going any further. As a young lad I had seen a local farmer call his cows for milking by blowing a trumpet, but to see a whole herd peering over a hedge obviously enjoying the performance of a full band was indeed a curious sight.

Led by the regimental goat it must have been impressive to see the whole battalion marching into Colchester. Shortly after our arrival, someone brought in a small press cutting that intimated that the Welch Regiment was being prepared for Korea. This leaked information finally decided the matter of our destination beyond whisper or dispute. Calling the whole battalion to order the CO addressed the men in a manner which made all the National Servicemen grin and groan simultaneously. Briefly he mentioned the newspaper article before boldly stating that he was 'pleased' to say it was correct – we were going to Korea.

To many of the National Servicemen and regulars, going to Korea was anything but good news, but most people were philosophical about it. During our last six weeks of training, Jim Sibeon, Lamacraft and I were given regimental signaller training, which we enjoyed. This also meant we were transferred to the Support Company Signal Platoon. We all found this new venture very interesting and soon we were operating 33 and 62 wireless sets as well as laying lines and rigging up field telephone exchanges. One of the curious things about the 33 sets was that they had the same frequency as television sets, and when we did exercises which involved passing through villages, there were many complaints from residents when our 'Baker', 'Dog' calls came out of their sets.

Climbing trees and telephone poles with crampons also appealed to our sense of adventure. Apart from their weight, the 33 sets were quite effective except in heavily wooded areas or in the lee of hills. We could often send calls 3 miles or so with these sets, and also receive strong signals from long distances. We could in some cases receive signals from radio stations and, unofficially, we were custodians of the latest cricket scores etc.

The 62 sets, which were usually used for static locations or perhaps in a Bren gun carrier, could often pick up fishing boats, police and other interesting transmissions. When we arrived in Korea the 62 sets were our main means of radio communication.

Within a few weeks of going on embarkation leave a tough, likeable character called Jim Swarbrick and I were picked to go on a stretcher-bearer course, with some lads from other regiments, some of whom were regulars. Jim and I had the distinction of coming out top in the exams and practicals and, thereafter, became firm friends. As I will describe later, Jim was to witness a very macabre and sad sight when we eventually arrived in Korea.

Chapter 6

Embarkation

Once the announcement that we were going to Korea was made, we were all given seventeen days leave so that we could say our fond farewell, which for some would be a final farewell.

For my parents it was a very worrying time because the health of my elder brother Jim was deteriorating. With a wife and young son to support, he was bravely trying to keep his electrical business going, but by the time I arrived he was failing fast.

As a healthy vigorous young man it seemed unreal that as I said goodbye to family and friends that I would be embarking on a voyage which would take me halfway round the world, and my father knew better than most the dangers I was likely to face. Looking back in hindsight I can now fully appreciate what an awful time it must have been for him and my mother. The thought of losing one son through ill health and perhaps one through conflict must have haunted my father. My mother in later life developed a condition where her hand would sometimes shake violently, apparently for no reason, but the real reason was the death of my brother and the strain of knowing I was fighting in a war 12,000 miles away. To me there was an air of excitement about meeting this challenge and somewhere deep down inside I was convinced I would survive.

Our embarkation leave seemed to melt away and before we knew it we were assembled at Southampton ready to embark on an old German battleship, the *Empire Fowey*. Captured during the Second World War, the battleship had been converted into a troopship which could clock up some 18 knots, so would get us to Korea in about a month.

As we left the quayside at Southampton, what seemed to be hundreds of mothers, fathers, wives, sweethearts and well-wishers crowded to see us off, but what a sad occasion it was. It was doubtless impressive to see the ship pull slowly away, but for those left on the quay it must have been slow agony as the ship weighed anchor and moved out to sea. Even brave men shed tears on such occasions. If you can avoid it, never go to see someone off who is leaving by ship. It is heartbreakingly slow and so irrevocably sad as the ship is manoeuvred from her berth and heads towards the horizon.

Once we were out at sea we had plenty of time to talk and think about the coming ordeal. The first few days were spent exploring and getting used to life at sea, and in no time at all we were heading into the Bay of Biscay. Famous for its mountainous rolling waves, Biscay soon had many of us feeling seasick. I was fortunate in that I was appointed a deck orderly, which meant I had to supervise and help scrub the deck we had been allocated. This work helped you forget the rolling ship and heavy seas, and apart from one occasion I quickly got my sea legs.

Even experienced sailors often get seasick in Biscay because the swirling currents cause large waves to form which don't actually break, but roll, taking the ship with them. These big waves roll even the longest ships, such that the propeller often comes out of the water and the vessel vibrates from end to end. After a week at sea I was tipped off that if you were a deck orderly you would be allowed ashore when we docked at the various ports on the way. This being so, I quite selflessly volunteered to be a deck orderly for the whole voyage. Lamacraft and Sibeon also joined our duty roster so that each day until deck inspection at 1000 hrs, we would scrub and scour every square inch of our deck, including tables, benches and anything which didn't move. At precisely the appointed hour the Battalion Adjutant or his deputy, and a senior naval officer, would come down and inspect every square inch of living space. If the slightest thing was out of place the senior officer would point to the nearest soldier and snap out the command, 'Soldier, pick up that matchstick!' or sweet wrapper, or whatever microscopic article offended his gaze. The slightest stain or spot of dust on the tables would also receive the same comment.

Whilst awaiting this daily inspection we would stand in a semi-circle facing the stairs which descended to our deck, and it became a source of amusement trying to guess who would be picked on by our eagle-eyed officers. This typical army/navy type of inspection procedure eventually led to one of the lads thinking up 'the matchstick ceremony'. So clean was the deck by inspection time that a matchstick left visible would stand out like a sore thumb, as they say. Just before the inspection team arrived, one of the lads would carefully lay one matchstick on the stairs to our deck. This was always done with great ceremony and then we would all put a few pence in the kitty, before nominating our candidate for picking it up. Down would come the retinue and, without fail, the senior officer would bark out the command. 'Soldier, pick up that matchstick – this floor is filthy!' Harmless fun really, but it helped the long days at sea pass more smoothly. Of course, we weren't green enough to play the game every day. That would have given the show away and we sometimes swapped the matchstick for a sweet wrapper or other minor blemish which would attract attention.

In the 1950s, very few people ever went abroad except as guests of HM armed forces, so it is not difficult to imagine our excitement at the prospect of a 12,000-mile journey by boat – very much a voyage into the unknown.

Our first port of call in the Mediterranean was Port Said, but we were not allowed to go ashore there. As we entered the Med we were fascinated to sail firstly past Gibraltar and then Malta, where the sun shone on the yellow rocks. We felt we were entering a new and magical world only previously glimpsed in books and, from time to time, at the cinema. Although we were disappointed at not going ashore at Port Said we were fascinated by the 'bum boats' which came alongside our ship, with an amazing array of goods for sale. A lively trade soon developed as money was lowered down in bags and all kinds of articles were sent up from the boats. By haggling, practically everyone chose something to send home and I bought some little highly decorated silk table mats. Quite a few of the keepsakes, such as cigarette cases, were made from hand-engraved aluminium and, in the years since, I have often seen these items at antique fairs, variously described, usually quite inaccurately.

The Egyptians themselves were dressed in intricately designed robes which seemed almost unreal to our inexperienced eyes.

During our stop at Port Said, I was appointed a deck orderly with quite wide powers to stop and report any serious misconduct. The ship's Captain and our own senior officers had made it quite plain that there were to be no missiles whatsoever thrown at the 'bum boats' and that all dealings had to be fair. I had the unenviable task of reporting some drunken sergeants throwing water and other objects at our Egyptian hosts. As regular visitors to Egypt, they had little respect for our trader friends, but whatever their motivation it was obvious from the dressing-down they got that such conduct in the 1950s was completely unacceptable. I thought there might have been some comeback on me, but much to my surprise the incident was never mentioned and the sergeants concerned took their roasting without complaint. Drink certainly does funny things to people and maybe these soldiers, who were probably ten years senior to us conscripts, were conditioned by memories of the British Empire when it was at its peak.

From Port Said we sailed down the Suez Canal which greatly impressed us – the sunsets had to be seen to be believed. Throughout the length of the canal, workers busied themselves with all kinds of tasks, sometimes taking time out to wave or shout a comment. On this part of our journey we spent many pleasant hours viewing the ever-changing scene. At one point we passed a group of soldiers who were working on the side of the canal and they couldn't resist shouting, 'Get some sand in your boots!' to which we replied, 'Get some snow in yours!' Although we were a long way from any such snow we were beginning to get the feel for what we were sailing into.

At various points we were amazed at the narrowness of the gap between the *Fowey* and the sides of the canal, so much so that at times we found it hard to believe we would actually get through, especially where locks were involved. By the time we reached Aden at the bottom of the Canal, the temperatures had risen into the high 90s Fahrenheit and we had to take salt tablets and drink gallons of lime juice. Which is why they call us 'limeys'. Never before had we encountered such heat – a steel ship isn't exactly the best place to experience near equator weather and our sweat cloths were in constant use. The poor old battalion goat was nearly expiring, much to the consternation of the Goat Corporal and others who saw him. When the Battalion was paraded with full honours and led by the Colonel, the battalion goat was bedecked with silver horns and a gold-braid coat to lead the Regiment on parade, so to see the battalion mascot so distressed did cause serious concerns.

As the *Empire Fowey* pulled into Aden harbour we were amazed to see little children of eight or ten years of age swimming out to meet us, even though we were half a mile from the shore. Treading water they called for us to throw coins to them, which we did. Diving like fish they would retrieve them and put them in their mouths until their cheeks were bulging. When they could cram no more in, they would swim back to the shoreline heading, it seemed to us, for a jetty. But as they neared it uniformed police appeared and started throwing rocks at them. We were not the least bit impressed with this behaviour and booed loudly, but it didn't make any difference. The children turned away and had to swim an extra 300yds or so to the beach where they were able to scamper away. It was said at the time that there were sharks around this part of the harbour so we couldn't help wondering what kind of a place this Aden was.

Twelve degrees from the equator, we knew one very significant fact and that was that it was the hottest place we had ever been to. Once ashore we made straight for the NAAFI where they had a fenced-off area of the sea which acted as a swimming pool, but we couldn't remain in it too long because the sun would fry us alive. We were told it was fenced off to keep sharks out, so there was no swimming in the open sea.

The old town of Aden was pretty down at heel and we were warned not to go into the poorest area. Needless to say we made for this part of town and as we strolled through it the curiosity of the locals just about matched our own. Very squalid, the crumbling buildings had poor, rough-looking men sat outside, but the children, although obviously undernourished, followed us laughing as they begged for coins. We duly supplied them with annas, an unusual coin with a hole in the middle, and they laughed louder as they scrabbled to pick them up. It is a marvellous thing that children the world over, even in the most dire situations, will react with smiles and gratitude to a simple act of kindness. At no time did we feel threatened, but then how many people would want to have a go at healthy soldiers, some standing 6ft tall?

Our spot of shore leave was soon over and we were once again back on our floating oven of a home, this time setting sail across the Arabian Sea. Our next port of call was to be Colombo, on the island of Ceylon now known as Sri Lanka, but before we pulled up anchor we were treated to one of those incidents that is disgusting but morbidly fascinating. Two of the regulars on our deck were known to be hard drinkers whenever the situation presented itself. It is a strange phenomenon that wherever you are around the world, and no matter how poor people are, they will find a way of making alcoholic drinks. Quite naturally we had been warned not to drink the local 'hooch', but equally quite naturally, it was very foreseeable that our heavy drinking friends would make it their business to search out the most potent local brew. Having found it, it would be inevitable that they would then down as much as possible in the shortest possible time. The result was two paralytic soldiers staggering aboard ship, unable to make sensible conversation or stand up without leaning on each other. Both made for their beds but the worst of the two literally fell into his bunk and passed out. The next thing we heard was him being sick all over his face and chest, but he was completely obvlivous to this involuntary retching. The next morning there was quite a crowd gathered round his bunk to watch him wake up. With his face caked in vomit, he first opened one eye and then the other. What a ghastly sight! He levered himself up onto one elbow before making the hilarious remark, 'What dirty bugger did this?' There was only one answer to that question and his mate, who was slightly less hung-over, told him. At this point, all those who had witnessed this horror story broke up and slowly walked away, shaking their heads in wonder and disbelief. How can getting totally legless through drink be classed as having a good time? I guess it is one of life's mysteries that will never be solved.

By the time we left Aden we were truly getting our sea legs, except for one or two individuals who were more or less permanently seasick. One of our mates, called Cutts, was so beset with this horrible complaint that he spent nearly all his time sat in the centre of the boat nibbling biscuits and sipping tea or water. Eating was a penance for him and most days he could barely raise a smile, which was not his usual style at all. Poor Cutts! The experience he was suffering was to make such a lasting impression on him that when his time came to leave Korea, he was trapped in a mental agony of half fear and half joy. As it turned out, his homeward journey did not affect him nearly so badly as this outward one. In those days there was no such thing as seasickness tablets, or at least, if there were, they weren't dished out to the troops.

At this stage of the voyage, I found myself doing a lot of serious reading. The ship had a good library and I found myself drawn to biographies and autobiographies with a few classic works thrown in – Aristotle and all that. When you are heading for serious danger it is surprising how thoughts of your own mortality sharpen the mind and leads your inner being to look for reasons why life is as it is. I felt that deep down inside I would survive, but even deeper down inside there were questions and answers I needed to resolve. As it was, the answers I wanted to some the questions were all waiting for me in North Korea.

The weather at this time was glorious and there was much to look at and learn as our ship ploughed through the high seas. I had heard about flying fish, but to actually see them was an amazing sight. I expected just one or two to surface for a few moments, but imagine the sight of up to sixty of these 'winged' curiosities, breaking through the waves at one time and then skimming the water for 50 or 60yds before disappearing. We could hardly believe our eyes. Like a flock of birds they kept formation and their wings and bodies shone like polished glass; definitely one of nature's miracles of adaptation.

Then there was the case of sea snakes. To see a 6–8ft snake swimming in a choppy sea is indeed a strange sight, which looks quite unnatural. But, of course, if there is one creature everyone likes to see it's the dolphin and during our journey we had several occasions when these joyous creatures led the ship, often diving underneath it and leaping for joy as they piloted us on our way. It was almost as if they were saying, 'Come and join us. This is our playground'. I thought then, as I think now, that these beautiful creatures should never be kept in captivity.

Another fascination which had to be seen to be believed was the appearance of fluorescent water. Every now and then a patch would appear off the bows of the ship and sparkle and dance like fire. This free education we were receiving would be paid for at a later date, but at the time we could only marvel at the experiences we were being introduced to.

Our next port of call, Colombo, proved to be on a very picturesque island, especially when seen from the sea. The beaches with their waving palms were very inviting, but we were told not to swim there because there was the chance that every now and again the sea would produce great rolling waves and the tides were very unpredictable. One thing for sure was that pineapples there were cheap and plentiful. We were hot and thirsty so it was quite natural that we should buy some and slake our thirst with great mouthfuls of this delicious fruit. In those days, particularly with memories of wartime food shortages still fresh in our minds, the only experience of pineapple was from a tin, so we did not realize that to eat them raw was to invite a sore tongue and lips. Such was the naivety of youth in those far-off days. I remember my tongue felt like it had been rubbed with a 12-inch rough file. You can't beat personal experience, but it comes at a price.

Strolling around the town we were impressed by the government buildings, but unfortunately we were not invited in for afternoon tea.

As we sailed away from this slice of paradise it was decided that we would have a boxing competition. Corporal Oram, my friend from Colchester days, was the organiser and trainer for this event so we knew the training would be tough, as indeed it was. Out on deck every morning, those of us who had enrolled for the contest were given a real gruelling. As training proceeded we were paired off for sparring and it soon became obvious that many of the lads were more than useful in the noble art of boxing.

I was matched against a Corporal Harris who, like me, was a light heavyweight. After a few rounds with him I was reasonably sure I could beat him, but I would have to be careful because what his windmill style lacked in skill, it made up in enthusiasm. Boxing is always a bit unpredictable and there is a big difference between sparring and an actual fight. Under my old friend Corporal Oram we sweated gallons as we exercised each morning. I think we all enjoyed the sparring, each of us taking on various opponents. I must admit I enjoyed the sparring, but I had no great ambition to really flatten my opponents. I had no doubt I could really hurt an opponent if I really cut loose, but as long as they kept the exchanges reasonable then I would do the same.

One of the strange things about boxing is that the better the opponent the more enjoyable the fight. Sparring with a good boxer you may get hit with hard sharp blows, but you usually find that the pair of you moved smoothly, almost to a rhythm, but if you sparred with a real novice then a lot of the time the fight would be awkward, and you were more likely to get a thumb in your eye or end up tripping over your opponent. Disjointed is a word that springs to mind.

Everyone was looking forward to the contest. The ring erected was very professional, and the stage was set for some good bouts. Unfortunately for me it was not to be. A few days before the fight I put my thumb out during a sparring session. It was an old injury I had received when I was only about twelve years old, but from time to time it would bother me if I seriously jarred it. During the war my father's brother Cyril had lost his wife due to illness, so for about two and a half years his two sons lived with us, until he remarried. Cyril had done some professional boxing when he was younger so that he had taken to giving me a few lessons. On one occasion he said he was going to show me how boxers use their heads. Ducking and weaving he invited me to try and hit him as hard as I could, but when I threw my hardest punch he pushed his head straight into it which nearly dislocated my thumb. It took weeks to get the swelling down. He was sorry, but he said that boxers sometimes pushed their head into a blow if it wasn't thrown properly in order to get inside. After that escapade my thumb was always a bit suspect and is still a bit fragile to this day. With me out of action my opponent was then matched against one of the ship's crew. From what I had seen of the sailor in action I didn't think this match was exactly even. The way the crew member moved and guarded himself made me think that he was no novice and had been in the ring many times before. Before the boxing tournament could take place, however, we had the pleasant experience of docking in Singapore.

Approaching from the sea, Singapore presents a fine sight. We sailed between attractive islands and what looked like plantations, with colonial-type villas and mansions dotted about, harking back to earlier times. As we neared land, however, we could see that the buildings were not quite as palatial as they seemed, but we were pretty sure it would be an exciting place to visit. As soon as the ship docked we headed straight for the line of trucks which would take us into town. Everyone was excited at the prospect of visiting this famous metropolis, but for one of the corporals the excitement was to be short-lived. As we pulled up to disperse, our unlucky Corporal was the first one to jump over the tailboard of the truck, but instead of landing on the road he disappeared into a deep, concrete monsoon gutter. Needless to say he was badly bruised and shaken and had to return to the ship for treatment. At the time it seemed strange to us that these enormous gutters would one day be full of water when the monsoons broke, but later, when we were entrenched in Korea, we were to learn what the word 'monsoon' really meant in practical terms – vertical rain that doesn't stop for days on end makes for a life that is definitely different.

Jim Sibeon, Jim Swarbrick, Lamacraft and myself all kept together and set off to explore the wonderland of activity and colour that is Singapore. One of the things which we found amusing was that if some of the shopkeepers couldn't get you to buy from them, they would offer to buy something off you. It could be your ring, your pen, or even your cap badge. It was certainly a different approach to what we were used to back home. This novel idea of commerce seemed to suit cheeky chappie Jim Sibeon, and in no time at all he was behind the counter in one shop meeting the shopkeeper's family. This particular establishment was owned by a Chinese gentleman, and yet here we were having a good laugh with a man whose relations might well be in the very army we were going to fight! The term 'multicultural' was never used in the 1950s but if it had been, Singapore would have qualified as a prime example: Malays, English, French, Chinese, Indians, Americans and many other nationalities all rubbed shoulders in this vibrant port.

As with many Eastern places, the marketplace by the docks was a hive of activity. Bright Chinese lanterns hung everywhere, giving the area a magical appearance, and the stallholders all seemed to have a permanent grin on their lean faces. Young men in uniform are always hungry so no sooner had we wandered our way into this arena of light and colour, than we found ourselves looking at a delightful cake stall. The cakes not only looked nice but were ridiculously cheap, so without hesitation I bought a few. They were as tasty as they looked and in no time at all we had nearly cleaned the stall out. The stallholder had a grin which spread from ear to ear, for no doubt this windfall of trade was more than welcome and as we prepared to leave, the stallholder gave me a couple of freebies in recognition of the trade I had brought him. I gave him a thumbs up which is universally recognized and we departed well satisfied.

In the 1950s, every place which was likely to have troops stationed there had a NAAFI. The one in Singapore was a particularly good one and very well known. One of its unique but comical features was its highly decorated toilet walls. You could spend quite a time reading the comments, poems, pictures and chit-chat that adorned the entrance area, but the most eye-catching phrase was circled with the simple words, 'A Happy Xmas to all our readers!' It was the biggest and funniest Christmas card I had ever seen.

The couple of days we spent in Singapore were indeed a very welcome break and recalling the highlights we experienced, one in particular could not have been funnier – that of the sight of Ishline Hughes and his mate Pritchard, racing around the streets pulling a rickshaw with the owner sat inside. Our shore leave passed all too quickly and soon we were back aboard ship heading away from the Malacca Straits, out into the South China Sea and towards Hong Kong.

It was at this time that the boxing tournament took place. There were some excellent bouts and what some contestants lacked in ring craft, they made up for in enthusiasm. Unfortunately for Corporal Harris, who was matched with an experienced crew member, he didn't appreciate he was up against a very good boxer. In the first round, Harris came out of his corner like a whirlwind, throwing punches at high speed, no doubt hoping to overwhelm his opponent. He seemed not to notice that his opponent blocked his punches with consummate ease, or that many of his punches missed by a mile. Just before the round ended the sailor released a wicked left hook, which just missed his chin by a whisker. Still not aware of the danger he was in, Harris continued to flail away. If he had been a bit less enthusiastic I think the sailor would have just boxed the match out, but as it was the sailor suddenly ended the match with another left hook, which this time found its mark. Poor Harris, despite his hopeful tactics, was the only one who had to suffer the indignation of being knocked out. The speed and style with which the fatal punch was delivered showed that the sailor was either a professional or a very good amateur. All the other fights were won on points, each fight being hard fought with little to choose between, so good was Corporal Oram's matchmaking. I was disappointed at not being able to fight but my turn was to come later, in Korea.

Boxing is a fine sport when carried out under controlled conditions with two equally matched opponents. It often creates a bond between opponents outside of the ring, because they respect their opponent's courage and skill after a close encounter. Even small-time amateur boxing teaches young people to give and take in a sporting manner.

As we left the Malacca Straits behind we began to realize that the next port of call would be our last before crossing the South China Sea to Pusan. As we neared Hong Kong the weather began to worsen which caused the ship to roll more and more, so that at times the boat fairly stood on end. This rolling of the ship was so pronounced that the washbasins would often spill their contents onto the floor. This spillage, in turn, caused many people to slip or fall in the washroom. It was under these conditions Jim Sibeon performed a feat never to be repeated. Jim had been having a shower, but as he stepped into the main area he suddenly lost his footing. Trying to regain his balance he did a Charlie Chaplin running-on-ice routine, before skidding backwards face down. Disaster loomed as he shot some 15ft towards an open toilet. Somehow or other he ended up with one foot either side of the toilet, unharmed. This display of unplanned acrobatics brought a few laughs from those who saw it, but it could easily have been a disaster. Under the slippery conditions described quite a few people required medical attention.

The weather calmed slightly as we neared Hong Kong and as we eased into the harbour we were greeted by an unbelievable sight. Every type of floating craft seemed to be manoeuvring in this magnificent harbour – how they didn't crashed into each other was a mystery to us landlubbers. Liners, battleships, Chinese junks, ferryboats and every other type of floating vessel continually criss-crossed this vibrant stretch of water, sometimes missing each other by mere inches. I had never seen anything like it in my life before and have never seen anything like it since. As our ship pulled in against a very long jetty a most amazing sight met our eyes. It was almost as if someone had stage-managed the enactment.

Near to our jetty was another jetty with an unusual end, which was obviously used for turning ships around after they had docked. As we watched, a large 30,000-ton vessel was approaching it. Gathered at the end were some forty or so Chinese dockers waiting to carry out various functions once the ship was in. Suddenly, they all started waving their arms and shouting, but about what we couldn't tell. Even more bizarre, the next thing we saw was this same crowd of workers racing like mad down the jetty, all trying to break the world record for sprinting. As fascinated and bemused onlookers we could not initially see what all the panic was due to, but then, like those on the quayside, we realized the ship coming in was moving too fast and at the wrong angle. When something weighing 30,000 tons impacts, even at slow speed, something has got to give. To our amazement what looked like a solid jetty suddenly crumpled like matchwood and disintegrated into the sea. What an incredible sight! The captain of the ship would no doubt be held accountable but to us, as observers, the scene seemed like an animated film which everyone found highly amusing. Years later, as a safety officer, I used to use this incident to illustrate the dangers of point loading.

Before we could go ashore to be let loose on Hong Kong (which I must remind the reader was a British colony at this time), we had to bull up and do a full ceremonial march through the town. It's called 'showing the flag'. With our goat mascot leading we marched in impressive style passing from the multi-coloured centre of the town through the poor quarters, where washing was strung in endless lines across buildings and streets. A festival of Britain in underpants! The residents were obviously impressed, but it was more than likely that Chinese spies would relay the fact that the Welsh were coming, which is no doubt what those in charge wanted. Having completed the circuit of the town we thought that would be it, but instead we were lined up and told to regroup in different combinations to those we had set off in. Most of the lads were surprised by this tactic, but I was certain I knew what it was all about. My father had told me that when he landed in Belgium during the First World War, after he had convalesced from a wound, he was surprised to find that not only did the contingent have to march round the town, but also had to repeat the exercise later during the night. The idea was to fool the enemy spies into thinking that more troops had landed than was actually the case. Our second march was almost certainly done for the same reason and once completed we were stood down and were free to explore this fascinating city.

Chinese silks, gaily coloured lanterns and shops bursting with goods of all kinds met our eyes, plus foods in strange colours and combinations. Full of colour and activity this exotic city was indeed a fairyland, the likes of which we had never seen or even imagined, particularly as the UK at the time still endured the restrictions of some wartime rationing. Once we had tasted the excitement and flavour of this bustling city we made for the NAAFI, which turned out to be a very luxurious affair, with oriental gardens and palm trees. I remember we all bought coconuts and hung them round our necks as we strolled through the canteen and gardens, before heading back to *Empire Fowey* to complete the final leg of our journey.

Our last port of call was Pusan which was now only five days away across the East China Sea. Once again, as we sailed out of Hong Kong harbour, we marvelled at the non-stop, criss-crossing traffic. As far as we could see the only rule which applied was, biggest takes preference.

Although we were becoming good sailors by now, we did not expect the rip-roaring towering waves which greeted us on the last leg of the voyage. Fierce winds whipped across the *Fowey* as she plied her way through the storms, trying to keep the speed at some 17 knots. When the winds were at their fiercest it was a case of hanging on to the nearest rail if you dared to venture up on deck. Quite a few people were sent skidding along the deck and several ended up in the ship's medical centre. The biggest danger from the stormy weather was usually encountered when you went on deck, and came up the stairs on the leeward side just as the boat rolled and the fierce wind gusted around your feet. Under these conditions you realized what the term 'hanging on' meant.

In the evenings we were often treated to film shows or the very old game, 'housey-housey', now called bingo. The sessions were well attended but many of us soon realized that the games were not exactly above board, as they say. Some of the regulars won far too often for it to be a game of genuine chance, but the 'housey-housey' games were nothing like as crooked as the brag and pontoon games run by Ishline Hughes and his mate Pritchard.

Jim Sibeon and I often watched these nose-scratching, ear-pulling and eye-blinking games, all the while wondering why some of the lads couldn't see these obvious signs. Ishline and Pritchard always shared their winnings, so I suppose that when Pritchard appeared to lose a few shillings the others thought it couldn't be a fix. Of course if Pritchard lost, Ishline won, and vice versa. One of our pals called Williams 75 got well and truly fleeced a few times before the penny dropped.

Most of the time life aboard was reasonably pleasant and for a ship crowded with 700–800 men there was relatively little friction. However, it would be unnatural for so many men to be packed into such a comparatively small space without there being a few flare-ups. There was talk of a knife being pulled in one incident but, fortunately, it didn't come to anything. However, I did have an experience at this time which has stayed with me all my life. Two days out from Pusan my boxing friend, Corporal Oram, came over to talk to me and for once he seemed in a very sullen mood, which was rare for him. He had said to me on a couple of occasions that he didn't think he would survive this trip, but I had not taken him seriously. As a regular, Corporal Oram had seen service in the Middle East when things were very unstable after the war, and he said he thought he had run his luck as far as it would go. On this particular occasion I was leaning on the rail of the ship when he came up to me. He told me that he had just written home, but that it was as if another hand was penning the letter – and that he signed off the letter by saying that this was the end of the line. I tried to make light of his remarks but there was inevitability about the way he spoke, such that I felt real unease and was unable to shake off his remarks. Some two weeks later, after we had moved into the front line, he was the first man to be killed by enemy action. A direct hit on the observation bunker he was in made his prediction come true. What a sad, sad loss. His death removed any doubts that this war was anything but a serious business.

I do not believe life is preordained but I do think that people do sometimes have insights into their own or another's mortality. Premonitions of things to come can sometimes be uncannily accurate.

Chapter 7

Korea – Pusan and Beyond

Almost exactly one month after setting sail from Southampton we landed in Korea, at the Port of Pusan. It was 10 November 1951. The *Empire Fowey* had battled its way through heat and winter storms averaging some 17 or 18 knots, which was pretty good going.

As we landed in this little-known country, halfway round the world from the UK, there was a real buzz of expectancy as we all tried to imagine what lay ahead of us. We had become used to life at sea, but now the time had come to face an unknown enemy. What would we find in Pusan? Housed in a transit camp just outside the old town itself, we had only a few days to explore this ancient city before we took a 48-hour train journey to Seoul. From there we would be transported across the 38th Parallel into North Korea, the peninsula having been divided into the northern and southern territories following the Second World War. From thence we would go into the line and on active service, whatever that meant.

In 1951, Pusan was a combination of very old oriental buildings in poor condition, surrounded by a shanty town which spread inland for about a mile. As you approached Pusan you could smell its presence long before you reached it. This ramshackle cardboard and scrap-material area was nothing like what we had ever seen or smelt before. It was quite nauseating, such that many of the lads held their noses or put handkerchiefs over their faces while walking through. This was humanity at its worst and I couldn't help wondering what had caused great powers to fight over such a wretched country.

As we left the shanty with its filthy stench we were quickly surrounded by children begging for anything we could give them: a coin, a sweet, a biscuit – anything was better than nothing. If we stood still some of these poor lost souls would start to clean our boots. Jim Lamacraft, Jim Sibeon and I could not but help these poor mites earn a few coins before they were chased away by the police. This was deprivation as we had never seen it before.

NORTH AND SOUTH KOREA

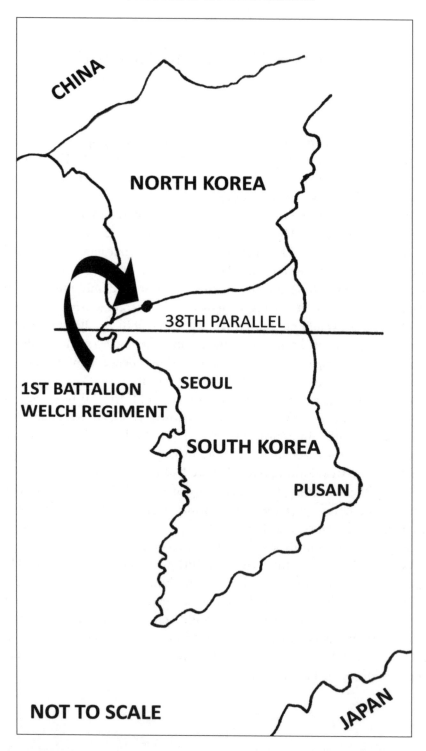

In the centre of the town was a very old rundown railway station and wherever we looked there were obvious signs of neglect and the resultant decay. A couple of visits to this end of the town were more than enough for most of the lads.

The older Koreans were very polite and in spite of their poor circumstances seemed to be most gracious in their manner, but they had a rather haunted look about them. Before we left their country I was to see that look many times. They knew why we were there, which I am sure they appreciated, but they must have wondered when they would get their country back and when would this nightmare of occupation end, and with what result? It was only a few years since the Japanese had departed after years of cruel domination. Later I was to be given a first-hand account of how cruel the Japanese had treated many Koreans. Even to this day, the Japanese are not particularly welcome in Korea and are viewed with suspicion. It is a strange paradox that many civilized nations can be as barbaric as they are cultured under some circumstances, with very little dividing the two.

After a few days in Pusan we took a very old and uncomfortable train to Seoul. Cramped on wooden seats for forty-eight hours is not exactly pleasant, and we found the hilly scenery quite pleasant but, on the whole, monotonous. The few small villages we stopped at were not much to look at, but almost invariably a handful of villagers turned out to try and sell a few bits and pieces. I bought a small ring stamped 'Korea' which I had for many years, but I think one of my sons eventually swapped it for something, as young lads do. I think it had been made from a brass nut, so poor were these mild-mannered people.

We were all very glad when we reached the station at Seoul, from where we were transferred to another transit camp. One of the curiosities of such a long journey was the endless succession of tiered paddy fields which dotted every hillside. There was also the almost unbelievable sight of what appeared to be little old men carrying absolutely enormous loads on simply constructed 'A' frames, the shoulder straps of which were made of platted rice stalks.

Seoul was only marginally better than Pusan. It certainly hadn't got the stench, but the dusty roads and unadorned buildings were not particularly impressive. American servicemen driving jeeps were in plentiful supply, but what their reasons were for dashing through the town we could only guess. I think that in many ways Seoul at that time had become a sort of giant transit camp due to its proximity to the border with North Korea.

In the few short days we were billeted in the camp at Seoul we were issued with our winter kit, which consisted of one very, very thick woollen pullover, under which we wore an army shirt and string vest. At that time our army greatcoats were to be our outer garment, but some six weeks later we were supplied with much more suitable winter gear which I will describe later. At the time of our initial equipping, we had no idea of what lay ahead of us during Korea's winter months, November to April. The lectures we received on frostbite were to prove very useful when we moved into the front line, but at the time they seemed a bit over the top – perhaps even unnecessary. Of course, real-life experience is a great teacher as we were to find out – it is one thing to talk of temperatures which are 40^0 below zero, and an entirely different matter to experience such conditions at first hand.

During our stay in transit we met several veterans of the conflict who were heading in the opposite direction to us. Quite naturally we were more than interested to hear what they thought of their experiences in this little known part of the world. One rather dry character summed up his perception of Korea in a rather crude way which, at the time, did have some measure of truth in it. When we asked him what he thought he said, 'Put it this way, when you get into the front line you are at the arse end of the world, and you are 200 miles up it! This country has six climates which makes it a bastard to live in. It has "two" hot, "two" cold and "two" wet!' He finished by saying, 'Always keep five rounds in your magazine and one up the spout. I'm going home,' he added, 'but all the best and keep your heads down.' Surely good sound advice, even if put a bit crudely.

Prior to being bundled into trucks to be taken up the line, we were given some more lectures on personal hygiene and methods of keeping warm, all very informative and useful but, as experience was to show, the Korean porters who worked for us were to prove by far the best source of practical guidance by example, when it came to basic living.

As a Regimental Signaller I was allocated to the Assault Pioneer Platoon whose job it was to both lay and remove mines or booby traps, blow up unexploded bombs and grenades etcetera, and act as a rifle platoon. The lads were all highly trained at making all kinds of explosives, using gun cotton and detonators, and were a great bunch to work with. Our first assignment when we moved into the line was to take over from some French Canadians who were dug in on the northern side of the 38th Parallel. To reach these positions we had to cross the Imjin River, which in many places flows at great speed through deep gorges. It had been said that no one had ever built a permanent bridge across the river which would withstand Korea's excessive weather. The Yanks not only took up this challenge but succeeded, and to make sure everyone knew of this achievement they had put up a very large sign indicating that they had conquered where others had failed. Not exactly the British way of doing things, but as one of the lads put it, 'Who cares!' In this largely uninhabited part of the world, I don't think notices of any kind had much meaning unless they indicated something nasty like 'MINES IN THIS AREA' or perhaps, 'BEWARE OF BOOBY TRAPS'.

Once we arrived at the front we were told that we were taking over a site which had been used by the French Canadians, but sorry to say we were not impressed by their standards of hygiene and general organization. Our first couple of weeks were spent digging 12ft deep swill pits to get rid of the rubbish they had amassed and the rats that went with piles of old food containers. The bunkers were very basic, even by our very inexperienced standards, and a massive effort was needed to make them more comfortable and easy to move about in. We soon knocked together seats and tables for our radio sets and the connecting trenches were deepened and cleaned.

It was at this time that we began to appreciate the Korean porters who were allocated to us. They helped with digging, carrying, laying wire, cooking and all the chores such as chopping wood. It must be said that their knowledge, along with their willingness to carry out any tasks without grumbling, impressed me greatly, as it did most of the lads. The porters were not allowed to carry arms but, other than that, they worked under the same regulations as we did. Conscripted, many of them had already been involved in active service. Most of them were countrymen, so they had a natural ability to make do and mend, such that an old box could soon become a chair, carefully smoothed with a broken bottle and stained with boot polish. They were without question a great asset to the Battalion and I became good friends with some of them. Honest, hardworking and resourceful, I developed a great respect for them. Many had the names Kim, Son and Chan, but I suspected they weren't their real names.

On our arrival at this site I was paired off with a Corporal C (I will not use his real name for reasons which will emerge later) and between us we built a command bunker which housed our telephone exchange, wireless sets and some of our personal gear. As Regimental Signallers we were at the heart of operations in our unit, because all messages came and went through us so we always knew what was going on or what was likely to happen. Adjacent to our bunker was a smaller one occupied by Major Parry who was the Support Company Commander. A half-a-bottle-a-night man, he was not the best officer I met in Korea, but I got on well enough with him.

During the first few weeks we lived partly off combat rations, known as C7s, and partly off food cooked in a field kitchen. C7s were cleverly designed, each box containing tins of meat, tinned fruit, biscuits, a mini tin opener, a plastic bag and one tin of food which had a fuse running through the centre of the tin, which once lit burned its way through the can in a minute or so to heat up the noodles or meat. These were very acceptable when we were on guard at night, but we had doubts about how long we would last if we were permanently living on these rations, which were meant to last twenty-four hours.

Every evening during the winter we were allowed a tot of rum, which was very acceptable but, quite naturally, some lads would store theirs up and have a binge. When this happened, it usually meant that once they became legless they would be pushed into their bunker and someone else would do their guard. They would have to make up for this missed duty at another time.

Although the hills we occupied in those first few weeks were semi-reserve positions, in that the enemy were about three quarters of a mile away across the valley, we knew they could attack at any time. Of course, dug in as we were gave us the opportunity to get used to the disciplines we would need when we moved nearer the front. Our machine guns and mortars were fired with live ammunition and we familiarized ourselves with the range and positions of enemy dugouts. By the time we had arrived in Korea, both sides were well dug in and a state of static warfare had developed, much the same as the First World War. Machine-gun fire, mortar shelling and from positions farther back, the 25-pounders, hammered away. Patrols probed the enemy and on occasion there would be company attacks. It was common talk that the Americans were attacked more than the Commonwealth battalions and my later experiences seemed to bear this out.

In a relatively short time the men got used to the screeching sound of outgoing shells as the 25-pounders were fired, but before we were to leave Korea we were to get used to the sound of incoming shells and become quite expert at judging where they would land. In some instances we could tell what type of shell or mortar bomb was targeting us. Almost every day American, Australian and British planes pounded the enemy, often flying quite low over our positions as they lined up the attack. To make sure we were not mistaken for the enemy, we were given large brightly coloured plastic markers to stake out on our hills on the opposite side from the enemy. The shapes we put out had to vary each day and in my platoon as Regimental Signaller, it was one of my jobs to do this. In spite of these precautions it did not stop the Americans strafing us on occasions. This they did rather enthusiastically at times and it was rumoured that they had, on occasions, bombed friendly troops, although this was never confirmed.

During this early settling-in period we soon came to appreciate what we had been told about sub-zero temperatures. The days might be bright and sunny with blue skies, but by 1600 hrs the temperature would drop dramatically to -8° or -12°. Later we were to experience the extreme of -45°, but for the time being -8° or less was more than cold enough when we were on guard duty or trying to sleep in our dugout with our boots on.

Whilst on active service we were given fifty free cigarettes a week and to those who smoked it was a valuable handout. In my case it meant nothing to me because I was a non-smoker, so I gave my ration to the Korean porters. They were highly delighted because they could barter them for all kinds of things. Giving one of the porters my round tin with fifty fags in was like giving them a hefty tip and it was much appreciated.

Most of our active-service wages were banked for us, but we were allocated a small amount of currency in the form of NAAFI 'baffs'. They were printed notes very much like real money, but they could only be used to buy NAAFI goods. If we wanted a few bars of chocolate etc. we could send an order back to one of the echelons and some days later the goods would be brought up by jeep. Korean money, the Yen, was almost valueless – there were 1,000 Yen to the £1. One or two lads bought some before they realized it couldn't be used, which was a great disappointment. Corporal C was one of the first into the exchange field and was delighted when he got a great fistful of notes for a tenner or so. I remember him coming into the bunker brandishing his new-found wealth, but when he tried to use it no one wanted to know. Ever the resourceful character that he was, he eventually got one of the Korean porters to buy him some hooch, when he was on leave, as they were allowed a week or so every six months. When the porter returned with the precious loot it had to be seen to be believed. The bottle containing the nectar of the Gods was about 18 inches long by 3 inches diameter. Probably made from rice, there was no doubt it would be potent and, as things turned out, lethal would have been a better description.

On the night the hooch arrived, Corporal C got the cook to join him in a celebration cup or two of the precious liquid, the both of them disappearing for an hour or so to enjoy their windfall. I was on duty until midnight on that particular day and was preparing to hand over when the Corporal staggered into the command bunker absolutely legless. He was definitely not in the land of the living, but rather alarmingly he was waving his rifle about mumbling something about Major Parry. This was potentially an explosive situation which could easily get out of hand, so I took the rifle off him and hid it under our wireless table, then escorted him to our bunker and shoved him into it. I laid him out as best I could and returned to duty, knowing that this was going to be a long night.

Major Parry must have heard or sensed something was not quite right and came into the command bunker looking for the Corporal. I made some excuses about a broken telephone line and busied myself around the telephones and wireless sets. I knew I would have to do Corporal C's stag (duty) that night, so when things had quietened down I left my post to find out what had happened to our cook. I soon found him a little way down the main communication trench near the field cookhouse. He looked terrible as he leaned against the sandbags. He hadn't drunk quite as much as Corporal C but, nevertheless he was anything but sober. I suggested I would get someone to do his guard duty, the idea being he could get his head down, but he said, 'If I go to sleep you won't get any breakfast and I will be in big trouble.' This being the case I had to accept that he would stay up all night and I would ply him with strong coffee at regular intervals. By daybreak, much to my relief, he was half sober, though he looked and acted somewhat in a trance-like state as he fried the bacon and eggs. He told me the sight and smell of preparing the breakfast nearly made him throw up, but somehow or other he got through the morning, mostly on automatic pilot.

Corporal C was entirely another matter. When I went to our bunker to wake him up and when he did eventually come round, I found myself looking into two blood-red eyes. What a strange sight. Years later when I worked as a safety officer, I found out this phenomenon was a symptom of toxic poisoning. He said he felt as if his head would explode and his mouth was like the bottom of a bird cage. By the look on his face he wasn't joking. Not surprisingly it took him several days to shake off the effects of his encounter with the bottle of Korean home brew. By coincidence, a few days later we received our weekly bulletin, which was handed out to give useful tips and advice to the troops. This particular issue warned that Korean hooch was dangerous and could cause blindness. Needless to say, Corporal C didn't need to read this particular pearl of wisdom – he was already an expert on the subject.

The bulletins I have referred to contained information on subjects such as which snakes were dangerous, how to purify water, how to guard against frostbite and how to keep rats out of the bunkers. This last one was always a potential problem, especially if there was any uncovered food around. Food for personal consumption was always kept in tins, but rats are opportunists and were ever present. To keep the infestation of rats to a minimum, holes to a depth of 10ft would be dug, into which waste food was thrown, and every day with the help of some petrol poured on top, the whole lot would be incinerated. When the hole was half full it would be in-filled with earth from the excavations and compacted down.

I suppose mice were a similar problem if allowed to multiply, but their diminutive size and appealing behaviour tended to make us treat them like pets rather than vermin. On many occasions when things were very quiet, usually in the early hours of the morning, one or more of these delicate little creatures would come scurrying along the logs in the roof of the bunker, descend onto the wireless table to examine any and everything which looked interesting. I don't think they were always after food, but quite often they would examine an object in a purely inquisitive manner. I remember one bright-eyed little traveller who came down to join me on my night watches, who seemed quite oblivious to my presence provided I didn't move quickly. On one occasion he climbed my tea mug, peered inside, groomed his whiskers nonchalantly, then moved on to other bits and pieces, to all of which he gave equal scrutiny. I didn't begrudge him his adventure, in fact I rated him good company, and I could always scour my cup with boiling water before I used it again. Rats, on the other hand, were a different proposition. No one liked them and many of them ended up skewered on bayonets, or were despatched by the rat poison we were issued with.

Later in the year, when I was posted to the mortar platoon, which at that time occupied a position on a hill just below the famous Hill 355 (Little Gibraltar), one of my mates in the Signals had a very nasty rat experience which I will describe later. It was the sort of experience that would make you cringe to even think of it. One of our sergeants also had a life-threatening experience related to rats which would be most unlikely to happen in normal life, both of these incidents clearly showing that the Chinese were not the only enemy.

The position we occupied in those first few weeks was greatly improved by the time we left, but we didn't know then that we would only be there for a few weeks. They did, however, give us experience in living the life that was to become our lot for the next eleven months. Quite quickly we learned that old machine-gun belts, woven on steel pickets, could make a good bed, and old supply boxes could be turned into chairs and tables. Local fir trees soon became the roof and walls of our bunkers and tin cans could become night burners or fancy candle holders. There was, however, one aspect of this life that caused quite a number of us to be concerned, and that was the need for a haircut. Under trench-like conditions you feel distinctly cleaner if you can get a regular haircut, but the battalion barber at that time was hard put to get round all the men once per month, which was not really adequate.

When we first arrived at our positions I noticed there were the remains of a small village with just a few Koreans still inhabiting it. Kim, one of our porters, said that the people there were all right, so I asked Kim what the word for hair was and, armed with the term morikarak, I ventured out to see if anyone could cut hair. The group of small huts was of the wattle and daub type, so to enter them was like stepping back in time. The walls were lined with platted rice stalks and only the most primitive of pans and cooking vessels lay about. Being amongst this small group of Koreans, who were mostly women, they all greeted me with smiles and obvious curiosity. Picking out one of the women who looked like a senior member of the group, I used my one

1ST WELCH BATTALION POSITIONS IN SAMICHON VALLEY, KOREA
24TH NOVEMBER 1951 TO 9TH MARCH 1952

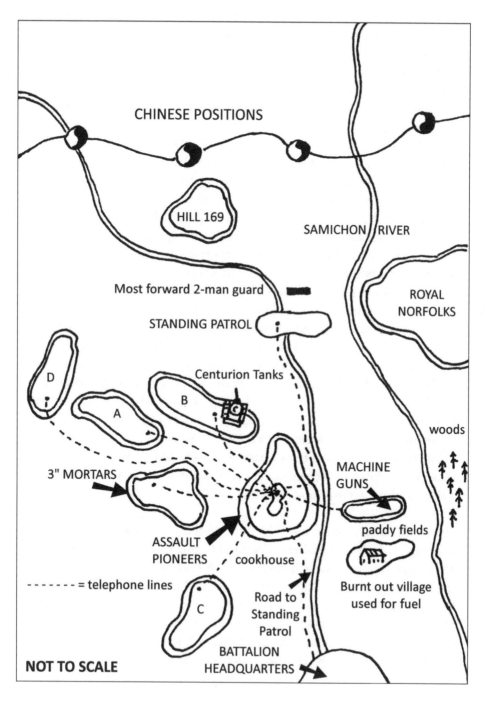

word of Korean, morikarak, and at the same time using my fingers like scissors indicating the cutting of hair. I waited for a reaction. The lady I was speaking to seemed to understand and disappeared outside, returning quite quickly with a middle-aged local man who seemed by his gestures to understand what I wanted. I nodded in agreement and pointed to my watch, indicating two o'clock in the afternoon, at the same time pointing to the top of our hill. He nodded in agreement, so I set off fairly confident I was going to get a haircut. Appointment confirmed – what could be easier. I trudged back up the hill to await the outcome of our meeting.

Sure enough, at two o'clock, my newly appointed barber appeared carrying a small sack in his hand. To smiles all round I sat down on one of the many petrol cans which were dotted around. Then, to the enjoyment of the interested audience which had now assembled, our Korean friend delved into his sack to bring out what looked like sheep shears. This caused instant laughter, accompanied by a series of wisecracks, but quite calmly my barber friend carried on with his preparations as if he had been doing this sort of work all his life. In for a penny, in for a pound, as they say, I signalled for him to begin.

Miracle of miracle, this slightly wizened figure began to snip my hair with style and ease which was obviously born of long practice. In no time at all I was cut and styled as good as if I had visited my barber back home. Laughter soon turned to grunts of approval and in no time at all a queue had formed. A couple of hours later half the company had been shorn, which impressed our Sergeant Major to the extent that my barber friend was appointed official barber to Support Company for the whole period we were in Korea.

The first few weeks in Korea passed quickly and we were soon on the move to establish ourselves in very forward positions in the Samichon Valley, and winter was now upon us.

On a cold, bright morning in December, the Assault Pioneer Platoon, together with their signallers, Corporal C and I, arrived on a hill some 500ft high, appropriately named Pioneer Hill, where we would spend the next four months. Prior to us, the hill had been occupied by Korean ROK soldiers – there had obviously been some heavy fighting on this promontory because many of the trees and bushes had been blasted clean away and a few stick grenades were found. Major Parry almost jumped 6ft in the air when one of the lads brought one to show him.

The ROK soldiers believed in living in a very Spartan manner without much shelter, so we immediately set to work making the rough and ready positions more secure and comfortable. Winter was setting in fast so we were soon appreciating what minus temperatures really felt like. Our command bunker was at the very crest of Pioneer Hill, but initially it was only a large hole in the ground, so the first priority was to roof it and get water and supplies to it. This was no mean feat because every item had to be manhandled to the top. Water and wood are heavy commodities so there was no need for any special physical training exercises once this work started. There was also the need to wire, and deepen and dig new communication trenches. Below Pioneer Hill the Samichon Valley snaked, away eventually disappearing amongst the Chinese position. Halfway across the valley was a natural ridge about 15–20ft high, and this was used as an advance warning station called the Standing Patrol, occupied by a section during the day but strengthened to a platoon every night. Because it was the most forward position in the Battalion and a very nerve-racking place to be, personnel were changed almost every week. Mines were laid in front of this position plus wiring, but it was frequently probed by the enemy, and our own patrols often passed through it when they were on similar missions. If the Chinese had put in a major attack in this area the Standing Patrol men would have had just about enough time to say, 'They're coming!'

Because Pioneer Hill was nearest to the patrol our lads did more than their share of manning it. As the signallers nearest to it, Corporal C and I had to make sure that the telephone line to it was always open. This not infrequently meant going out at night to service the line if it got shelled. I also visited it on numerous occasions with our officer when he went to see how the troops were getting on during the long night vigils. In no-man's land there was a very important hill called 169 and near to it there was a pair of hills, code named 'Twin Tits'. Around these hills a lot of activity was to take place in the four months we were positioned on Pioneer Hill. When we first arrived on our positions, Hill 169 was occupied by our lads in the daytime and the Chinese at night, but gradually the Chinese dug right into it and as I will describe later, refused to be forced off in spite of horrific bombardments.

Within a few weeks of moving in our bunker had been roofed with logs from trees across the valley, plus some taken from an abandoned burnt-out village close by. All of this work meant we had to do a lot of chopping, splitting and carrying of large loads of wood, which most of the lads enjoyed. However, it was the Korean porters who showed us how to use an axe properly and how to open a split in a tree trunk. By placing a small piece of wood in the split, then following the grain, slowly but surely, the split would open up which would eventually allow even large trees to be halved and quartered. Patience allied to an easy, relaxed chopping action was also shown to be superior to our initial brute strength and ignorance approach. This hard work gave a feeling of satisfaction as well as a feeling of security as the bunkers took on a permanent look with log-lined walls and heavily logged roofs, onto which was laid a thick coat of rice straw, with soil on the top. In some cases tarpaulins were run out over the top and secured with a covering of rocks, this being the last layer to take the impact of any shells or mortar bombs before they penetrated.

Halfway down our hill a field cookhouse was built which was very acceptable to everyone, because cooked meals were infinitely better than C7 field rations. Dug into the hillside next to the cookhouse was a tunnel-type mess bunker which could hold about twenty-five men and this was a good meeting point at breakfast and the evening meal. News and banter would greet the day in this construction when we went for breakfast and one of the Liverpool lads (I think his name was Talbot) often used to read out his poems which were generally of a pen-portrait type. Poetry of this type is often in the same category as a ventriloquist's doll in that things can be said which would not be possible in everyday conversation. No one was safe from our resident poet's sharp wit.

During the early period of our bedding in, a very amusing situation developed between our Sergeant Major Walsh and the Korean porters. When we first arrived on the hill, our food was dished out each day in the form of C7 rations, plus what the cook could rustle up. The porters had the same rations as us until Sergeant Major Walsh in his wisdom decided they would have to supply their own. Big mistake! In typical army style he bluntly told them of his decision, but straightaway they began to dispute it with exclamations of 'Number ten, number ten!' The porters eventually went into a huddle and after a short discussion emerged with smiles and nods to each other. Without a further word they all returned to the jobs they had been doing, but with a difference. The work was still smooth, accurate and well done, but the speed had reduced to what could be called 'slow motion'. Every now and then the word 'chop chop' would be exclaimed and each time other porters would smile and nod. The Sergeant Major tried some army-style chivvying, but the porters just carried on sleepwalking as if they couldn't hear or understand what he was getting excited about. Eventually, after an hour or so of this go-slow response, Sergeant Major Walsh gave in and told the cook to give them some food. Meal finished, it was as if someone had pushed the gear lever up a couple of notches and the pace of work returned to normal and with smiles and thumbs up the porters were heard to say, 'Sergeant Major Walsh – number one.'

As a result of this incident we had all learned that 'chop chop' meant food, and our Sergeant Major realized it was easier to get co-operation if he didn't try to make our eastern friends lose face.

It was about this time that I was privileged to witness a most unusual incident the likes of which I have never seen before or since. On the particular day in question, I was returning to Pioneer Hill after repairing a telephone line, when I came across three Korean ROK soldiers standing in a paddy field at the side of the dust-track road I was walking along. Two of the men, who looked like privates, were stood to attention facing each other about a foot apart. The officer was obviously giving them a right old dressing-down. Suddenly he barked out a command and one of the men gave the other man an almighty smack across the face. The recipient of this smack never batted an eyelid. The officer then barked out the same command and soldier number two gave the man facing him an equally nasty smack. The officer finally barked another command and the two privates shook hands, saluted the officer and were marched away.

What would a psychologist make of that? Perhaps I had witnessed the way to stop wars. Get the two most warmongering politicians together and let them have the same treatment? I had heard the ROK soldiers were tough and ready for anything, but the incident I had just witnessed really did give me food for thought.

As we settled into our new positions, it became colder every day. By midday the sky would be a brilliant blue and the sun would begin to take the frozen dew off the grass, but by 1500 hrs the temperature would begin to fall rapidly as icy winds began to whip against the face and hands so that by 1700 or 1800 hrs, minus temperatures would be the norm and anything left uncovered would be frozen solid. Even rifles and Bren guns would freeze up in five or ten minutes if not cocked, even though they had antifreeze oil on them.

When on guard in the early hours you could feel your feet begin to stick to the ground if you stood still for a few minutes. If nature called in the middle of the night you could use one of several latrines which dotted the hillside, but they were very basic, merely a deep hole partly covered by planks with a box-type toilet on top. For this operation everyone would take a blanket with them to wrap round themselves once their trousers were down. This eventually led to a common saying which was used when someone was looking for someone else at night.

'Have you seen Jones around?'

'I think it was him going for a crap with a blanket round him.'

Before the winter was out, however, we had experienced temperatures of -45⁰.

On the plus side it was during the first few weeks at our new position that we were issued with our proper full winter kit. Starting from the feet, and working upwards, it consisted of a pair of commando boots, with nylon mesh inserts which allowed a cushion of air under the feet to keep them warm. Conversely, in summer these inner soles kept the feet cool. Wool socks were topped with long-john underpants, over which we then had what could be described as tracksuit bottoms. Over these went wind- and waterproof trousers. On the top half was worn a string vest, over which was worn an ordinary vest, army shirt, woollen pullover and rain- and windproof three-quarter-length jacket. On night guard this was topped by a fur-lined parka coat which zipped down and fastened under your crotch. The hood on it was wired to allow you to pull it in to cover most of your face. This last feature was very good, but could not be fully used when on guard because you were unable to hear and see properly. Even with this protective gear on, if you took your gloves off at night your hands would become numb in seconds. If anyone lost a parka there would be a court of inquiry, army style. I only knew of one case where this happened, but the senior NCO concerned was a wily old campaigner called Colour Sergeant Francis. He was a very likeable character who became our NCO in charge for a period whilst on Pioneer Hill. As I will describe later, he talked his way out of his difficulty when his parka went missing.

Some days it was so cold when you went to breakfast that unless we dipped our knife in our boiling tea to spread our butter quickly, it would go solid. We would then have to drink our tea quickly or it too would go cold and freeze over. The food was plentiful and before the winter was out almost everyone had put at least a stone on. It was soon lost, however, when the summer came, but that's another story.

A novelty which occurred at this time was that of freezing and shaping hair. If we washed our hair in the open using water which was piping hot, then only half dried it, it would go very stiff and could be bent into funny shapes. Some lads who still had longish hair could make themselves look like pantomime dames, or something equally comical, much to everyone's amusement. The novelty of weird hairstyles soon wore off, however, but it does give some idea of how cold it was and the extent to which a few of the troops would go in order to keep their mates' spirits up.

The first six weeks in our new positions were very tough for Corporal C and myself because we were one signaller short, which meant that the two of us had to give 24-hour cover on the telephone exchange and wireless sets. We did this by doing twenty-four hours on and six hours off. I would go on duty at 2400 hrs one night until 2400 hrs the next night, then Corporal C would do the same. To make matters worse, for the first three weeks, we only had an old crystal set which meant we couldn't take our eyes off it, because when someone rang the jack connectors lit up, but there was no ringing sound. Sometimes in the early hours when we needed matchsticks to keep our eyes open, we could easily imagine we had seen the light flicker even when it didn't. Then at other times our mind would tell us it had not rung through when it had. This could easily be the case if someone at the other end only gave a quick ring which would produce a mere flicker. We were more than glad to see the back of this obsolete piece of equipment from the Second World War.

During the long night watches one of our duties was to change the guard every two hours and make them a cup of tea before they turned in. We also had what at first seemed a rather amusing task but which was, in fact, a serious business and that was to inspect each guard's nose and ears to make sure there were no signs of frostbite. When the temperatures are well below zero certain parts of the body can easily lose their feeling, whereas the person concerned is oblivious of how cold his ears, feet or nose have become. This procedure was well founded because the lads would be so tired when they came off guard, they would not be fully aware of the potential problem and we all had orders to sleep with our boots on. If it was considered that their feet or ears were rather numb, I would get them to warm them before they turned in. On occasions, I would do someone's guard whilst they kept an eye on the telephone and wireless sets. I would only be just outside the command bunker in the stand-to bay if anyone rang, so it was easy for me to nip in and answer the call. I did this mainly to keep myself awake, because while their guard duty was for two hours, I was on duty all night. Such is life!

During those harsh cold nights we learned things which no amount of book learning can prepare or make one fully understand. Sometimes, when we were really tired and cold whilst on guard, our knees would buckle and we would be startled for a second until we realized we had momentarily gone to sleep, standing up. It was at this time that we realized how easy it would be to die of exposure – just close your eyes, nod off and never wake up, and this was so in some cultures in times past. Placing an old worn-out Eskimo on an ice floe and giving him a ceremonial send-off was, perhaps, not as barbaric as it sounded to westerners living in comfort.

During the endless long night watches I began to read a small book which had the 'Sermon on the Mount' in it, and the more I read it the more I became impressed with the timeless pearls of wisdom in it. It was as if someone had switched on a light and illuminated this ancient text. I had always attended church until my early teens, but had not grasped the full depth of much that I had read or heard. The insight and revelation which came to me during those long nights has stayed with me throughout my life, and has been a great source of inspiration and comfort. Now, in my old age, I still believe that the message Christ gave on the mount was the most important ever given to mankind. In that short passage contained in Matthew, there lies the wisdom of the ages. How strange that I should have to travel halfway round the world and be engaged in a war I knew little about, to gain the valuable insights contained in this New Testament passage.

Those first four months we spent in the Samichon Valley were full of light and shade. I am sure no one who experienced those days has ever forgotten them.

Only a short while after we arrived in our new positions, an incident occurred which put everyone on their toes, as they say. On the particular night in question, one of the lads decided to go outside his bunker for a pee (the cold usually accelerates this necessity), but on popping his head out of the bunker he was confronted by a Chinese soldier squatting on the edge of the trench. 'Enemy!' he yelled as the shock spurred him into high-speed action and he dived back into the bunker to get his rifle, but by the time he emerged ready to do battle, the unwelcome guest had faded into the night. Our command bunker was nearest to the incident so quite naturally we were alerted first. Once informed of the situation, Major Parry seemed to panic a bit and immediately gave the order for some 2-inch mortar flares to be fired. So rushed was this action that one of the lads burnt his hand on the mortar and the flares revealed nothing, save our own position. Shortly after this incident, the CO gave an order: 'Flares are not to be used because they give away our location. Since you know your position better than the enemy, in reality flares help the enemy more than yourselves.' This incident caused a major 'stand to' and next day we could see the marks in the snow where our unwelcome visitor had been, but whatever his person or purpose, he had vanished off our site. Everyone was put on their toes, however, but none more so than Private Johnson.

Although a nice lad, Johnson really was definitely not soldier material. He was by nature of a very nervous disposition and there was no doubt he was finding the ordeal of taking part in the Korean War more than could be reasonably expected of him. His mate who shared his bunker had told me that Johnson was so agitated he had filled his pillow case in his sleeping bag with grenades. Definitely not the norm. This was carrying the idea of being prepared at all times to an almost comical level – leastways, that's what most of us thought at that time. However, an incident occurred at that time which brought Johnson's nervousness into full focus such that Sergeant Major Walsh was involved. Quite often at the evening stand-to I would accompany Sergeant Major Walsh on his round of the platoon to make sure everyone was fully alert. On this particular occasion as we approached Johnson he called out the necessary 'halt' and gave the first half of the password. As it happened the Sergeant Major was slow answering up so I called out, 'It's Nev, with Sergeant Major Walsh.' Out of the dark came an ominous click – one up the spout. At this I gave the password and moved forward quickly. Johnson held his ground until we were right on him.

At this point Sergeant Major Walsh moved close to Johnson and asked the very pertinent question, 'What would you have done if we hadn't answered up, Johnson?'

'Shot you,' came back the reply.

This may have been a copybook answer, but in real-life action conditions, we frequently halted people and recognized them by their voices or some wisecrack remark. On searching his bunker, Sergeant Major Walsh was not impressed by Johnson's pillowcase stuffed with hand grenades. I tried to put a good word in for this misplaced, agitated lad, but Walsh was having none of it. 'You're for the Standing Patrol tomorrow,' he told Johnson as we passed on, but I couldn't help thinking that whilst this was a typical army solution to this apparent problem of an unsoldierly National Serviceman, in this case it was a mistake. Two days after this incident Sergeant Jones and I were on the hill talking when, in broad daylight, we saw a lone figure walking along the snaking road from the Standing Patrol which was the most forward position in the Battalion and, thereby, the most dangerous. Dug in on a natural ridge of land halfway between ourselves and the Chinese on the other side of the valley, the early warning position would have been a suicide position if a big attack had been launched. Despite the wire and mines in front of it, it was often probed by Chinese. To drive or walk along the road to it in daylight was to invite trouble. Both Sergeant Jones and I recognized it was Johnson who was wending his way back, so we trotted down the hill to meet him.

Sergeant Jones asked the obvious question, 'Where are you going Johnson?' Eyes sunken, face ashen, Johnson looked like a man with one foot in the grave. He was obviously a broken man.

His reply was simple but profound. 'Home,' he said.

Sergeant Jones and I looked at each other and there was no need for words. 'Keep an eye on him for a minute,' said the Sergeant, 'whilst I get a couple of lads to see him back to HQ,' which was about a mile or so down the bulldozed road we were on.

What happened to our friend after that I never knew, but we never saw him again. No doubt the Army would find him a suitable job to serve out his time. Whatever his future might have held, we all felt sorry for him for there was no suggestion of cowardice. Who knows what a man can stand when he's faced with a war situation? Of course, in much earlier conflicts the Army's view of this incident would have been summed up as dereliction of duty – and Johnson would have been called a deserter.

My father had told me that when he was in France, he had witnessed the horrific sight of one of his comrades being shot in front of the whole battalion. To make matters worse my father had shared a hut with the man's brother. When the execution was carried out the whole battalion had swayed, he told me. Father's opinion was that if one man had broken ranks the whole battalion would have mutinied and possibly killed the officers. He also told me that on more than one occasion, soldiers who had seen a lot of action and had reached breaking point had asked him to shoot them through the foot, using a sandbag so as not to show close-range burns. He had not obliged, but knew cases where this had happened. War can be a very heart-rending experience which often causes men to behave in ways which they would never do in civvy street. For some it exposes strengths and abilities they never knew they had, but for others it can be a crushing and demeaning experience which can ruin or even snuff out their lives completely.

On the subject of self-inflicted wounds, it was strongly rumoured that our battalion barber had opted for the Sten gun way out of this war, shortly after we arrived on Pioneer Hill. He had made it known that he didn't rate this Korean War and that one way or another he was for out. Whilst on guard one night he did get shot in the foot with his own Sten gun, but his story that it was an accident was accepted. He said that he had forgotten to apply his safety catch and that his gun had fallen from his arm causing it to fire a couple of rounds, one of which penetrated his boot. This was just about plausible because Sten guns work on a blowback action which could cause them to fire if dropped. However, at breakfast time the general opinion was that it happened 'accidentally on purpose', but in the dark no one could be sure. There was, however, another incident of this type which was tragic in the extreme.

On the day in question I received a telephone call from one of my signaller mates in B Company, who were on a hill to our left. Jim Swarbrick was the stalwart Yorkshireman with whom I had become very friendly while back in the UK. Jim and I had come top of the group on a stretcher-bearer course which was made up of servicemen from various battalions. Both of us had enjoyed the two-week course and, thereafter, often went out together as part of a group. Every now and then Jim and I would have a chat over the phone in order to keep up with the local news. However, when Jim made contact on this particular occasion it was obvious he was very upset and stressed. One of his mates had been shot. Jim didn't want to explain the circumstances down the line, but said he would come over later to give us the full story.

Jim Swarbrick was one of those individuals who was very solid and dependable so we knew that if he was upset something out of the ordinary must have happened, and so it turned out to be. Jim's mate had, apparently, been cleaning his Sten gun in the bunker, and on completing this exercise he had shouldered the gun and bent down to step outside. Unfortunately, he had forgotten to put the safety catch on before putting the magazine on, and as he ducked down the gun slipped off his shoulder, hit the floor and went off. The bullet shot him straight through the heart and Jim, who was nearby, arrived at his friend's side just in time to see him die.

I was not surprised when Jim exploded with the words, 'The only good Chinese is a dead one!' Before National Service I doubt if he ever imagined witnessing such a terrible sight or responding in such a manner. My own view of this war was slightly less cryptic but, nevertheless, I was determined to stay alive, and do whatever I had to, to achieve that goal.

News of my brother's death from kidney failure brought on by diabetes had made me doubly concerned to survive. Without the life-saving transplant surgery that is performed today, it was inevitable he would die. If the news of his death was a blow to me, what must it have been like for my mother and father? One son dead and the other 12,000 miles away in Korea, facing danger they could only guess at.

I had never questioned the government's right to send me to Korea, but I did not have any feelings of hate for the Chinese. In fact, I could easily believe that they were conscripts like us, fighting a war they didn't understand. This being the case survival was the aim. So as a vigorous young man I was determined to outlive the war, no matter what it took to do so.

Chapter 8

Danger Everywhere

Whilst in the line we had the unpleasant experience of sleeping with our clothes on, including our boots, but like a lot of experiences which are not exactly normal, in war you have to get used to them – which we did. In the case of sleeping in boots, it meant that we had to wash our feet and change socks daily if problems were to be avoided. Most of us also had strip-down washes every day in order to avoid bugs, and in my own case I never had any trouble with this particular enemy all the time I was in Korea. I think the delousing powder we were given also played its part. Prevention is definitely better than cure.

The accidental death of a comrade by his own gun heightened our awareness of the need to be disciplined when handling small arms. Rifles, Bren guns, Sten guns and grenades were all readily available on our positions each day, and we frequently had to handle them whilst on guard duty. In a relatively short space of time, however, I was involved in three incidents, two of which came close to me losing my life.

Each morning one of my first tasks after stand-down was to clean my rifle and pull it through. Once cleaned the drill was to put the empty magazine on the rifle and operate the bolt before pointing the rifle up in the air and pressing the trigger. I had done this operation many times but on this particular day when I pointed the rifle up in the air and pressed the trigger a bullet was discharged through the roof of the bunker. This more than surprised me because I was always careful about removing the five rounds from the magazine when I took it off the rifle before cleaning. Somehow I had missed a bullet on this occasion. Sergeant Jones came rushing into the bunker to see what had happened, but when I explained he nodded wisely and remarked, 'Drills do pay off.'

The second incident was much more serious and involved our officer in charge, Lieutenant Wild, and Sergeant Jones. During the winter we had several officers take charge of the Assault Pioneer Platoon, each having a very different style and personality. It was said that Lieutenant Wild had come to us from a Canadian outfit but whatever his background he was a likeable man, although a bit gung-ho, as they say – hat on one side, moustache and .38 pistol slung a bit low. I got on well with him, but I think he considered Korea and the war as Wyatt Earp country, in need of 'sorting out'. When he disappeared off site, as he did most days, he rarely told me where he was going, but when he returned his conversation suggested he had been seeing and talking to Americans or Canadians. On the particular day in question, when he returned to the bunker about 1600 hrs he was highly excited. To Sergeant Jones's and my surprise he was brandishing an American .45 pistol, which was not British Army issue. We were even more surprised when he told us he had swapped his issue .38 pistol for the .45 he was holding. The bullets for the .45 were much bigger than those for the .38, and he lost no time in showing us how the pistol butt loaded into the .45.

Sergeant Jones was rather reserved about this swap, because I think he realized it was not a very legal or sensible idea. However, Lieutenant Wild took the bullet magazine out of the butt, dropped the pistol on one of the picket beds and invited Sergeant Jones to examine it while he went into his bunker for a few minutes. On examination the Sergeant commented that the barrel was very worn and, out of curiosity, he slid the magazine into the butt, then placed the pistol back on the bed. As an afterthought he took the loaded magazine out of the butt and placed it away from the pistol. He had no sooner done this than Lieutenant Wild strode back into the bunker, picked up the pistol, pointed it at my chest and pressed the trigger. What a stupid, thoughtless act. A few seconds before this act of bravado, or whatever, the pistol had been loaded.

'You stupid bloody idiot,' I exploded.

'That pistol was loaded a few seconds ago,' interrupted Sergeant Jones.

Lieutenant Wild blanched as he realized what he might have done. In the Army it is a chargeable offence to even point a gun at anyone, unless it is in earnest, let alone pull the trigger.

'You could have killed me a few moments ago!' I shouted at him. 'What the bloody hell do you think you're playing at?'

Utterly confused, Wild made a quick apology and left the command bunker for his own adjoining accommodation. This was one occasion when I could have called him anything and there would have been no repercussions. If he had shot me he would have been court-martialled and probably jailed. As it was, when Sergeant Jones asked me what I was going to do, I said something to the effect that we had come here to fight

Chinese and not each other, but the Lieutenant was lucky I hadn't planted one on him.

Sergeant Jones was relieved to know the incident was closed, but he went in to see Lieutenant Wild and later Wild came out and made an abject apology, which I accepted. Later, the Lieutenant confided to me that he thought I was going to punch him when the incident happened, to which I replied that it was a close thing.

There was, however, a lighter side to this incident in that a few days later Wild came into the bunker to offer me a pair of size 10, Canadian, knee-length, lumberjack-type boots. This peace offering was highly acceptable because there was no doubt these boots were the finest footwear around. Very hard to come by it was only the likes of colour sergeants and a few officers who had enough pull to prize a pair of these boots from the Canadians. On and off I wore those boots for the whole time I was in Korea and was able to pass them on to our trusted porter Kim when we eventually left for home. Fording streams, climbing hillsides, pushing through undergrowth, those jackboots were worth their weight in gold, as they say. Wherever I went with them on someone was sure to ask how I got them. Although the pistol incident was closed, I did notice that a few days later Lieutenant Wild was once again wearing his .38 pistol. I think Sergeant Jones had put him straight on the legalities, but whatever the reason he never mentioned the subject of the .45, nor did we ever see it again.

As can often happen with a close encounter of this kind, Lieutenant Wild and I became good friends and not infrequently he would give me the doubtful privilege of going with him to the Standing Patrol, to make sure they were OK and that morale was good. The lads were always glad to see us out there in no-man's land and we usually took them a few fags and sweets which were gratefully received.

Before the winter was out I had good reason to remember some of my visits to the Standing Patrol and I have no doubt many of the lads who spent time there would never forget the experience. It was also the case that many of the patrols which went out into enemy territory had to pass through and return via the Standing Patrol. As I will recount later, one of the patrols turned out to be an enemy patrol which had got lost.

Because our position was nearest to this patrol and we had the only telephone line to it, which we had to keep open twenty-four hours a day, we not only maintained it but were privileged to some of the conversations reported by our returning patrols. Shortly after the .45 pistol incident, I was on duty one day when I received a phone call from the CO asking for Lieutenant Wild. As was often the case I didn't know where he had gone so I tried to bluff the CO by telling him I would get in contact with him and get him to ring back. The CO was a very forthright and shrewd man and immediately picked up on my remark.

'What you mean, Signaller, is that you do not know where he is – do you?'

I gave a sort of half-hearted, 'I will soon find him, sir.'

The CO replied in a brusque manner, 'When he comes back get him to phone me, and the next time I ask you where he is, answer, "I will get him right away", or, "I don't know where he is".' With that he slammed the phone down.

A good man the CO, was always sharp and on the ball. If he came on site he would always ask the relevant questions such as, 'Where are the enemy?' 'Is the food OK?' 'Do you get your mail?' 'Where are your hand grenades?' If things were not quite right he would soon get someone to rectify them. When Lieutenant Wild came back later that day I told him the CO wanted him and when I put him through I could tell by his face that the CO was treading on his toes a bit. Surprise, surprise. After that phone call he always told me where he was going when he went out.

Of course, officers in charge of the Assault Pioneer Platoon were always busy visiting the lads as they went about their business on other sites, disarming or blowing up mines or grenades, or in other cases blasting trenches in the rock-hard ground. Shortly after the pistol episode, I had one very amusing incident when visiting the Standing Patrol with Lieutenant Wild.

On the particular night in question it was very dark and cold so that the midnight walk to the Standing Patrol seemed unusually long. But we were eventually halted which meant we had reached our destination. Manning the Bund, as it was called, was very nerve-racking because the Chinese often probed it. Once inside the bunker which was established there we had a cup of tea and a chat before setting off to see the two lads who were in a slit trench at the most forward position, some 200yds in front of the isolated bunker. As we approached these remote characters we were once again halted and asked for the password. I answered up but as we approached the soldiers in the slit trench, we bent down to see their faces and I could hardly contain my laughter. The face looking up was none other than Smith 99. Smithy had not long before left the Assault Pioneers to join the Mechanical Transport Section (MT) and at the time had boasted no one would ever see him directly in the front line again –

and here he was, the most forward lad in the Battalion.

'What happened?' I whispered, as I bent down.

'Driving too fast,' came the reply.

We gave him and his mate some chocolate before leaving, but I couldn't help wondering what magical force arranged these remarkable experiences. There is an old saying that both good luck and bad luck come in threes, and so it was for me at the time of the .45 incident.

The second near miss came a few days later when I was descending the hill to the cookhouse, which was a couple of hundred feet below the summit. Being pretty fit in those days I used to go down part of the hill at high speed, using the mountaineering technique for traversing scree. This requires that you lean well back, dig your heels in and then descend in a sort of running and jumping action. About 100ft from the cookhouse was a trench which ran round the hill and when I reached that point I would jump it and carry on. On this particular day I jumped it with ease but exactly what happened I do not know, because the next second I was hurtling down the hill, head tucked in, grabbing right and left at bushes as I sped by. Somehow or other I eventually grasped one and found myself facing up the hill. Gingerly I picked myself up and to my amazement found that I was unscathed except for a few scratches, but when I looked up I could hardly believe the distance I had fallen, some 50ft, all in a few seconds. As I gathered myself together Sergeant Jones and several of the lads came rushing up, all of them looking very concerned. They couldn't believe their eyes when they saw I was all right. Initially they were still very concerned but once they realized I was unhurt then the sympathy really flowed in.

'I know you're keen to be first for tea,' someone quipped, 'but this is ridiculous.' Then someone came up with an equally caring remark. 'That was brilliant Nev, but I didn't see the first bit, could you do it again?'

Whilst at tea the sympathy flowed in and for the next half day or so my acrobatics provided some light relief. Eventually I had to explain to everyone that what they had seen wasn't by any means my best effort, because I could do the same thing and actually change my mind in mid-air, so I didn't need their sympathy. These remarks slowed down the flow of jokes and asides, but the incident was made to measure for a bit of ribbing.

The third incident to complete my hat-trick of misfortunes at this time started when one afternoon the telephone line to our F Echelon supply base went down. At about 1530 hrs on this rather wet afternoon I set off across country to find and repair the offending break in our line. To do this you had to pick up the line outside the bunker and then, by giving it a pull, follow it across country. At times it would disappear in the undergrowth which slowed you down as you pulled and searched for the next bit of line. The C Company Echelon was about 2 miles away, so by the time I reached the break, which was literally at their end, it had become dark and the rain was getting heavier and heavier. I was a bit annoyed when I found the break because the signallers at the Echelon were supposed to check their end for at least half a mile or so. When I found the ends they were well and truly chewed up, probably by a tank or Bren gun carrier. Whatever the reason for the severance there was no doubt I would have to get some cable to make up the lost portion. Considering the fact that this break should have been sorted out by the Echelon lads, I had no difficulty in getting the wire, along with a good brew of tea and a few biscuits. Having completed the repair and exchanged a bit of news with the lads, I set off on my wet and windy journey, but by now the weather was really atrocious. Even though I knew the route across country, it was so pitch black that I frequently stumbled and in several places I had to negotiate wire fences. In such inclement weather a couple of miles seem like an endless journey. Eventually I reached a spot where I could just make out the outline of our hill. Rifle on my shoulder, holding a field telephone, soaking wet and weary, I found myself plodding up the hill with just one thought in mind: a cup of tea, something to eat and bed. Suddenly a voice in the dark barked out, 'Halt – who goes there?' 'Blue,' I answered. The return answer should have been 'Lagoon', but instead I heard the voice of Private Hewson sing out, 'Moon, I saw you standing alone'. This was, of course, a verse from a popular song of the 1950s, and with that we both burst out laughing. I had a few words with him and then carried on up the hill.

Suddenly I was falling through space to land flat on my back in one of the many slit trenches which adorned our site. Momentarily stunned, I lay there in the wet mud just gazing upwards, when suddenly the clouds parted slightly and I could see stars. Strangely enough, at that rather low moment in my life, I suddenly felt that someone up there was watching me and that I was cared for – an experience never to be forgotten. Slowly I raised myself and plodded silently up the hill to our command bunker. As I entered I could tell by the look on the faces of the others that I must have looked a sorry sight. Wet, muddy and weary! Corporal C immediately poured my rum ration into my water bottle top while Sergeant Jones got me a hot drink. He also got the primus going so that I could stand over it to dry out a bit.

Things were beginning to look up, but as I picked my rum ration up, the water bottle which was attached to it jerked my hand and most of it went

The Korean engineer and his wife who the author and his wife met on a train in Engleberge, Switzerland in 2000, over fifty years after the end of the Korean War. He thanked the author for helping to save his country from communism.

This picture of one man from each battalion in the Commonwealth Division was taken by General Cassels before he left for England. L to R: Indian regt, the northern (1st Welsh) Canadian regt, English regt, Australian regt, New Zealand regt (this is not Scottish regt

The author and his wife on top of Mount Titlis in Engleberge, Switzerland after meeting the Korean engineer and his wife.

Photo of platoon after initial training passing-out parade. The author is first left, second row down.

Studio photo of the author after six weeks training.

The author, Jim Sibeon and Jim Lamacraft in battle training area, East Wretham, Norfolk, May 1951.

1st Battalion The Welch Regiment marching into Colchester after a 60-mile trek from the battle training area in Norfolk.

Outside the NAAFI on Colombo, October 1951. L to R: the author, Jim Lamacraft, Jim Swarbrick, Williams 85 and Jim Sibeon.

Outside the NAAFI in Hong Kong. L to R: Jim Sibeon, the author, Williams 85 and Jim Swarbrick.

Pioneer Hill command bunker sketch, Christmas 1951.

Command Bunker Pioneer Hill Korea 1952

L to R: Chang, Kim, the author and Hewson, Pioneer Hill, Christmas 1952.

L to R: the author, Chang, (not known), Dixon, Hewson, Kim, (not known), Obrien.

HEAD DRESS KOREA 1952

WINTER.

PONCHO

FUR CAP WITH EAR MUFFS

WIRED HOOD ON PARKER JACKET

WOOL HAT

HELMET WITH CAMOUFLAGE

SUMMER

NO HEAD COVER

HATS HORRIBLE

BERET

LEAF HAT

Various types of headgear worn in Korea.

Sketch of Hill 355 from across the valley (Little Gibraltar). Note the 3″ mortars in the middle distance, May 1952.

HILL 355 KOREA 1952

View across 3″ mortar position, June 1952.

Unknown American soldier on 3″ mortar position near Hill 355.

Diving for cover as a shell lands on the 3″ mortar bomb bay when the author and two others were doing some wiring. Note that the rocks on the bay set the shell off before it could penetrate.

Sketch showing typical arrangement of bunkers, trenches and various other important items on a mortar position in Korea. A. 3″ mortar bay. B. Blasted tree with washing on it. C. Bunker. D. Slit trench. E. Bunker sandbags. F. Bunker chimney. G. Rocks on bunker roof. H. Blanket doorway. I. Petrol can. J. Cast-iron heated washing bowl. K. Barbed wire. L. Axe and shovel. M. Soldier in monsoon kit. N. Monsoon drain. O. Vehicle bogged down. P. Swill pit. Q. Latrine. R. Urinal.

The author on leave in Tokyo, June 1952.

Sketch done by street artist in Tokyo, June 1952.

June 27th 1952
TOKYO JAPAN

The author outside the command bunker, 3" mortar position, June 1952. Note the large loudspeaker for relaying music to the lads.

Pusan Military Cemetery in which the author's fallen comrades are buried

M.V. "DEVONSHIRE"

The famous old warhorse, *Devonshire*, which transported the author home in November 1952.

The author and his wife Joan on their wedding day, 9 June 1956.

on the floor. Never mind, I thought, as I stood over the primus savouring the warmth which was also starting to dry my windproof jacket, I'll soon be in bed. But who should come into the bunker at that moment? Who else but our half-a-bottle-of-whisky-per-night Major Parry! 'That primus is noisy,' he complained as he came in, but the looks on the faces of those present must have spoken more than words, because he disappeared back into his bunker (which adjoined ours) mumbling, 'Be as quick as you can.'

I was so cheesed off by his miserable attitude I kicked the primus into the corner (not my usual style) and got into my picket and machine-gun belt bed just as I was. Within minutes I had fallen into a deep dreamless sleep, and when I awoke some hours later I was practically dry from my own body heat. What a blessing is sleep.

Before the winter was out, there would be many scenarios like the one just described, but there were also many compensating days when the skies were blue as blue and the sun shone. At such times when things were quiet it was hard to believe there was a war going on at all.

During conflict, hope, fear, joy, sadness and thoughts of home all mingle, sometimes in the most unexpected ways. One thing was for sure, anyone involved in the Korean War would have indelible memories imprinted on their minds.

As regimental signallers we were often privy to conversations of a confidential nature. The field telephone service of that time worked on the basis of lines laid from company to company, with each company having its own signallers who were allocated by the Signals Sergeant at Battalion HQ. In the case of Support Company, which consisted of the Assault Pioneers, 3-inch Mortars, MT Section, Supply Depot and Machine-Gun Platoon, each had its own signallers. Each signaller had a battery-operated 33 set (range about 2–3 miles), a 62 set (10-mile range or more) and a telephone exchange which could often accommodate twelve or so lines. When someone rang an exchange a little flap would drop and when we plugged in the jack (master plug) we could talk to the caller. When we found out who he wanted to talk to we could plug his jack into that station, but if we left our own jack plug in the caller's we could listen in. Not that we would, unless of course we were one of the 99.9 per cent of the company who were curious.

Shortly after the revolver incident, I was on duty in the command bunker when Corporal C, who had just taken a call, signalled me over to listen in on a call from our CO to Major Parry. The Corporal held the phone earpiece so that we could both listen to what was a remarkable conversation, which went something like this.

'Hello Bob,' said the CO, 'How are you enjoying things up there?'

'Very well,' said Parry.

'Well, that's not the impression I have formed,' said the CO.

There was a pregnant pause before a rather nervous Parry replied, 'Why is that sir?'

'Well,' said the CO, 'I see that you have put in for the course on Chinese, which I put out to all officers.'

'That's right,' said the Major. 'I used to be good at languages.'

There was an ominous pause this time before the CO delivered his knockout blow. 'Bob,' he said, 'I thought you would have realized that the suggested course in Chinese was only a hoax to find out which of my officers was not happy to be in the front line. I hardly expected one of my senior officers to put in for the suggested course.' This statement was followed by a deathly silence as the CO finished the conversation by saying, 'Bob, we will have to talk,' and the click of the phone as the handset was slammed down.

Corporal C and I quickly unplugged the call, but after hearing that very serious conversation, we knew that Major Parry would soon be leaving us. And so it was. A few days later he packed all his belongings and disappeared to become a liaison officer working behind the line. For an infantry officer to be given such a post was really a demotion, but we were fairly sure Major Parry would be a happier man doing that job. Looking back, I suppose it must have been very hard for a rather frail man in his forties to cope with the rigours of a Korean winter in the conditions we had to endure. His regular whisky tippling would only have deadened the pain in a temporary sort of way, but whatever the whys and wherefores of the case, we were glad to see him go.

Before Major Parry left, however, we were joined by Lieutenant Mennell who was a most likeable and lively character. Sergeant Walsh was also replaced and a Colour Sergeant Francis joined our unit. With Mennell and Francis in charge, things took a definite turn for the better. In no time at all, both of these intelligent and resourceful characters started to make their presence felt. Lieutenant Wild was also transferred and despatched to a rifle company, and at the same time a Private Domonic was commandeered to make our signal strength up to three. This last posting was more than welcome, because it made our 24-hour manning of the telephone and wireless station somewhat more reasonable. A cockney lad, Domonic was a very likeable character with a good sense of humour and he fitted in well.

Chapter 9

Creature Comforts

Prior to Domonic's arrival, Corporal C and I were nearly worn down by the long tedious hours manning the phone and wireless sets, plus the never-ending tasks of fetching and carrying water and wood. To get sufficient wood for our converted ammunition box stove, we had to cross the valley below us and visit the abandoned village. The small houses had been constructed in the traditional method and wood was plentiful, but it was a rare old slog to carry a hundredweight load up some 500ft. To load the logs we used an 'A' frame device which was similar to that which supports a rucksack, but the Korean porters used their own home-made version, which was made of branches with straps of platted rice stalks.

Rather amusingly I noticed that Chan and Kim, two of our trusted porters, always made sure that whatever I carried in the way of wood, they carried a little bit more. Always willing to take part in a bit of harmless fun, I decided on a particular day that I would test their Korean pride to the full. Being pretty fit in those days, I knew I could manage a really heavy load, probably in the region of 130lb or so. As I loaded up I could see Chan eyeing me with a half-hidden grin. As his load increased so mine went higher. Kim, who was a bit older than either of us, realized early on what the joke was and when we reached about a hundredweight, he dropped out of this strongman contest. Kim and Chan had a slight advantage over me in that they only had to carry their loads as far as the cookhouse which was halfway up the hill but, nevertheless, it needed a strenuous effort to get the load up onto our backs.

As we trudged back to our positions our feet sank deep into the boggy paddy fields, but when we reached the cookhouse a mock cheer went up as the lads recognized the unannounced competition. Putting our loads down the lads couldn't resist a shower of jokes, which was often the case when something unusual happened. 'First time I've seen a forest on someone's back,' chimed in Hewson, one of our Liverpool wits, followed by various other remarks. 'I'll bet you could carry a good load if you were really trying,' someone else called out before the inevitable mock sympathy started. 'Poor buggers, they ought to get an MID. You shouldn't laugh at people who don't know any better.'

Thinking ahead, and in order to be able to pick up my load after I had had my tea, I went into one of the trenches and deposited the wood on the edge. Sergeant Jones, who shared our command bunker, called across that he would carry the load the last 200ft because, like the rest of the lads, he was quite impressed by our efforts. After tea everyone gathered round to watch our Sergeant do his bit, but to everyone's delight, our willing Sergeant found he couldn't even get the load up on his back. He was a short, stocky character, but his fitness was just not up to this particular challenge. 'Sorry, Nev,' he said, 'I'm afraid this has to be all yours.' And so it was. Joke over, Chan, Kim and I kept our loads to a more reasonable weight thereafter, but we remained firm friends throughout my time in Korea.

Diligent, honest, willing men, the longer I knew them the more I admired their simple, ever-useful attitude to life. In their skilled and resourceful hands, discarded articles and containers could become useful items. They recycled many items, and as a tradesman myself I greatly admired their skilful application to the tasks they undertook. Very often something made of wood was finished by burning boot polish into it so that the final result looked like a Waring & Gillow mahogany special. On many occasions I used the method they used to produce a night light from a tin can and a bit of hessian sack, once I had seen it crafted, as illustrated below.

Making a night light

Before I saw Kim in action I thought I knew how to use an axe because as a fourteen year old in the war, I had chopped fir trees down, and turned them into logs for our winter fire. However, when Kim first saw me in action he smiled and gently took the axe off me to demonstrate the easy way to split a tree. I soon realized what I thought was axe work was really a method based on brute force and ignorance, but Kim's method was something entirely different. Although already mentioned, I must elaborate a little on his skill. When splitting a tree trunk Kim would first of all turn the log around to study the grain. With a relaxed, easy stroke he would drive the axe into a natural split in the grain. He would place a small chip in the groove, then do exactly the same thing again just below the cut. In no time at all what seemed an almost impenetrable tree trunk would begin to open up and, once a major split was established, he would repeat the process to quarter and halve the pieces split off. His effortless relaxed strokes with the axe were far more accurate and effective than our mighty (axe stuck/can't pull it out) swings. Working with nature rather than against it is something the Western world has largely forgotten.

To produce heat inside the bunkers, quite a few men fashioned a wood-burning stove, by taking a steel ammunition box and cutting the lid in half so that one side could be lifted. The sides and top would be punched with holes and at the end of the box a chimney was made using steel mortar-bomb carrying cases. The chimney was fed through the bunker roof and when the box was filled with wood all that was needed to start it was a small can with petrol in, placed under the wood. Once a match was thrown into the petrol there would be a 'whoof' as the whole thing ignited and in no time at all you had a glowing box radiating welcome heat. Petrol to light it was not a problem because cans of it were readily available on site.

Home-made stove

This arrangement was very effective as long as you could get plenty of wood, but there was another system that was officially issued under the name of 'space heater'. In theory, this device was just what was needed to heat the bunkers, but in practice it was often not as good as the many improvised versions. The space heater consisted of a steel drum about 18 inches in diameter, with a central steel chimney which went through the bunker roof. The problem was that the little petrol-fed valve was not well designed and often gave an erratic feed of fuel. This could cause the heater to start to vaporize and the chimney would start to glow red hot. As the roofs of the bunkers usually had a layer of straw in them, once the chimney started to funnel the vaporized petrol fumes, you couldn't stop it until it had burned itself right up and out of the chimney, which caused many bunkers to catch fire, and a few men got burned enough to need treatment.

One of the most important priorities for a platoon or company, when first arriving on a new site, was to construct some kind of toilet. The method we used in Korea was to dig a deep pit, across which planks were laid. At regular intervals the planks would have holes in them and over these holes a box-type arrangement was placed, the top of which had a suitable sit-upon hole cut in it. Every day, petrol was poured into the pit and set on fire. Once the pit reached half full it was filled in and a new pit was dug. Sacking on poles was used to give a little privacy, but the whole arrangement was really most inadequate. Corporal C and I were not over impressed with this set-up, so in our spare time we set about carving some proper wooden seats and then, using broken glass, we smoothed them before applying burnt boot polish to give them a French polish-type finish. This activity encouraged others to clean up the whole latrine area such that we could boast the best facilities in the Battalion. Most visitors to our site were highly impressed with our efforts and many were the jokes passed around when our toilets were visited. This resulted in several little notices being posted. 'Wipe your feet when entering this establishment!' 'Please put the seat down when you have finished.' Hygiene is a very important factor in war situations and plays an important part in keeping men fit as well as helping morale.

There is no doubt that the Korean porters played a very significant part in helping our soldiers dig, lay wire, cook and make best use of the primitive facilities available to us. As in most wars the men who did a lot of the support tasks and hard graft, rather than the actual fighting, gained very little recognition during and after the war. My father told me that Chinese labourers were a great help in the First World War, but they got little mention or recompense. Things hadn't changed much.

Chapter 10

The Battle Continues and Voices from Home

As we got settled in to Pioneer Hill we became more and proficient in carrying out our daily tasks, and there was no doubt that it was necessary. The temperatures were well below zero and by late December the war had become very much a static operation, similar to that documented in other conflicts.

Both sides were well dug in and much of the activity revolved around shelling and patrol work. One of the focal points for us in the Samichon Valley was Hill 169, which was very isolated in no–man's land. When we first arrived it was mainly occupied by our troops during the day, but bit by bit the Chinese dug their way into it at night. Gradually we noticed that bunker doorways began to appear on the hill and even when our Centurion tanks moved up to plant amazingly accurate shells right into the openings, it didn't seem to make much difference.

To examine the extent of the Chinese diggings, our people decided to send out patrols to reconnoitre the situation and my old mate Jim Sibeon was one of those selected for this dangerous mission. Being a daylight patrol there was little if any cover and Jim told me later that they were only halfway up the hill when they were fired upon. Apparently, two Chinese soldiers had been left behind in a slit trench with the purpose of harassing our patrols, and this they did very well. The Chinese used what were called 'burp guns', which could fire eighty rounds a minute, so two men in a trench could put down significant firepower. Jim said that no one was injured, but that he had never hit the ground so fast in his life. He didn't need telling to fire back at the enemy, and I quote, 'I fired the fastest twenty rounds I had ever fired, but God knows where they went.' At least they had the desired effect of frightening the enemy off. This allowed the patrol to examine the bunkers under construction and, as suspected, the Chinese were aiming to establish themselves permanently.

This information was fed back to HQ and shortly afterwards the Assault Pioneers were given the unenviable task of blowing the bunkers up. This they did by wrapping cortex and gun cotton round the supports, plus a charge to lift the roofs, so that when the charges were detonated, the roof lifted and the supports sheared. This system was written up and later used elsewhere.

The lads who carried out this exercise in broad daylight were at great risk and I thought someone should have got a decoration out of it. The lads themselves were glad to get out of the situation in one piece and said it was a rather eerie situation going into these bunkers, not knowing if they would meet any enemy. Sad to say a few days later the Chinese were back on the hill, digging their way right through it. A tenacious nation the Chinese!

This situation did not please our CO and as we neared Christmas it was arranged at 0900 hrs on a designated morning, Hill 169 would become the focus for a 'Hate Target'. This meant that on that particular morning every gun in the Division was ranged up on this hill ready to fire at a given signal. Light and heavy machine guns, 25-pounders, 3-inch mortars, Centurion tank guns – just about anything which could reach Hill 169. Just before the appointed time, a reconnaissance aircraft flew over and dropped a red marker bomb onto the hill, and then another aircraft followed up by dropping two 500lb bombs. When they impacted our hill fairly shook, so what it was like for the Chinese we could only guess. Then, at precisely 0900 hrs, the whole Division opened up on Hate Target 169 and the air was full of screaming metal as every battalion pounded away for something like an hour. When the barrage stopped we could see that part of the top of the hill had been completely blown off. It must have been awful for the Chinese, but one thing was for sure: they were exceptionally tough and determined and within a few days signs of reoccupation appeared.

Later in the year, when we moved to a new position, we were destined to get a taste of our own medicine, but that is another story.

On a lighter note it was about this time that a concert party came out from the UK to entertain the troops. The show was a few miles behind the line, at one of the HQs, and we were taken, a few at a time, to see it. To experience some kind of light entertainment at this stage in hostilities, particularly so close to Christmas, was a great morale booster and we really appreciated the effort made by the stars to travel this far.

One of the singers was the famous Bill Johnson of the musical, *Annie Get Your Gun*. It was said that as the principal actor/singer, he had performed the show some thousand times and there was no doubt he was a very popular and world-class singer. His rendering of the famous negro spiritual, 'Old Man River', was cheered to the echo and he was encored numerous times. There were several other well-known artists including the actress and comedian Beryl Reid, who had a very high profile career at that time. Artists who go into war zones to give of their time and talents do a wonderful service, which lifts the spirits of even the hardest men, easing tensions and bringing a touch of 'normality' to the troops.

Later in the year we had a visit from that great comic, Ted Ray. I will never forget his two opening jokes. They absolutely brought the house down, as they say. At the time of his visit the railways had just been nationalized and as Ted bounced on the stage he opened his act by telling us that he had been sent out by the government to give us this important information. 'Now lads,' he said, 'I have been sent here to tell you that we all own a part of British Rail.' He followed this up with the punchline, 'And I've got the toilets at Barnsley.' Was there ever a better one liner to beat that? It was the thought of someone travelling 12,000 miles to Korea and then another 200 to reach us in order to give us that information.

A day after the Ted Ray show I was asked to go back and see the show again. This seemed a strange request, but I was told that some Americans were being invited to see him and there was concern that they might play up a bit. The idea was that we should mingle amongst the Americans to be a sort of calming influence. They need not have worried. Ted Ray had learned his craft in places like Birkenhead, where you were likely to get a week's groceries thrown at you if you were not up to scratch.

Sure enough, however, one of the Yanks threw a coin onto the stage when Ted appeared, but he treated it very casually as he picked it up, pretended to bite it, then announced that it was a dud. He followed this up by saying that there were times when a penny was very useful. He went on to explain that when he had arrived for the performance he had just had a long journey over a bumpy road, so that by the time he arrived he was busting for a pee. When he asked someone where the urinals were he was directed to an old mortar tube stuck in the ground halfway up the hill. It was true that this was a method of accommodating the need, the tube being partly buried in a soakaway of stones, but it was also true that some of the tubes were used as chimneys for bunkers. You can guess what happened. Ted used the tube and three Korean porters staggered out of the bunker shouting, 'Number Ten – Number Ten!' What made many of us laugh so loud about this joke was not only the thought of it happening, but also the fact that it had happened. Colour Sergeant Francis told us he had made the same mistake on one of our sites, and I am sure that he was not the only one to do so.

Ted Ray gave a brilliant performance and when I got back from Korea I wrote him a thank-you letter to which I received a very courteous reply. It was said that when Ted was at the height of his fame he could, without any rehearsal, perform for several hours, so great was his repertoire of jokes. In those days his radio show, *Ray's a Laugh*, was the number one show on the wireless. Unlike many modern comedians he didn't need to swear or use crude material to get a laugh – one of life's gentlemen.

On the subject of comedy we were not without our share of comedians in the Battalion. Some of the Liverpool lads were natural comics and one particular lad could always be relied on to liven up the proceedings. Hewson was a very versatile soldier who could be equally at home in the machine-gun section or acting as a jeep driver for one of the officers. He was initially attached to the Assault Pioneers, but was often loaned to the machine-gun section. When Hewson was helping out in that section he used to come to our cookhouse for his meals and was always pulling the cook's leg about the food. 'Morning, cook,' he would say as he queued for his meal. 'That was a great dinner you cooked last night.' Although slightly suspicious of praise from our 'mutual friend', the cook would nevertheless smile with some measure of pride at the unexpected praise. Then would come the punchline. 'You are the only cook I know who can make rubber taste like steak!' Everyone would have a good laugh and the cook would grin ruefully.

On one occasion the cook's helper, Kim, asked Hewson to teach him a couple of number one words in English. Hewson thought for a moment, then pointed to a little clearing on the hillside which had a small hump on it. 'That is called a snooze box,' said Hewson. This description was hilarious because in reality these small clearings with their little humps were really graves where the dead were buried in the sitting position, a very strange custom by our standards. Hewson followed this description with an equally bizarre word. 'A very good word to use,' he informed Kim, 'is the word ambidextrous.' Kim knew there was some kind of joke in this situation, but was happy to play along. Hewson then had Kim practise these two important words, but in the case of the word ambidextrous, he could only manage 'ambidextrix', which when said caused more laughter than ambidextrous. Armed with these two words, Kim was encouraged to say them as the lads filed past to collect their meals. Each time Kim would say number one words 'snooze box', at the same time pointing to the hillside graves. Those of us who had heard the build-up to this performance stood back and enjoyed the various reactions to this pearl of wisdom. Each time Kim would follow up this initial remark with his other newly acquired addition to his vocabulary. 'Very ambidextrix,' he would say as he slapped a ladle full of food on his next customer's mess tin.

The recipients of this comedy invariably stuck their thumbs up and grinned or laughed out loud. By the time everyone in the platoon was served, they were all pointing to the graves and calling 'snooze box', followed by a thumbs up. Because the reaction of everyone was so positive, thereafter Kim frequently used these two words to the great amusement of everyone. Snooze box and ambidextrix soon became the platoon's catchphrase and were used many times thereafter.

Hewson also had a mate, Talbot, referred to earlier, who was not only a comic but could write comic verse. Much to everyone's amusement he would do pen portraits of everyone including the NCOs, but because they were in verse he could get away with all kinds of backhand compliments which would not normally be acceptable. Our resident poet would often pen a poem when something unusual happened and at breakfast he would pin it up on one of the open cookhouse bunker supports.

Our poet's efforts were well appreciated by everyone except Sergeant Berry, who was in charge of the machine guns at that time. He was a rather dour character and although he would have his breakfast with his lads and the Assault Pioneers, he didn't seem to fit in too well. When one of the poems was read out, he could usually be relied on to have a bit of a moan. That fact that no one else was in tune with him must have penetrated to some degree, because it became noticeable that he did not generally join in the conversations and banter that would occur at mealtimes. Word had it that on his own site he was a bit of a bully and, as anyone who has been on active service knows, bullying does not go down well.

One breakfast time a group of the lads led by Hewson got a conversation going about patrol work. They made sure that their voices just about carried as far as Sergeant Berry, who was sitting nearby. 'It was certainly hard, frightening work,' said Hewson, 'but I've heard that some

NCOs who went on patrol, and others who didn't, had enemies in front and behind them.' Sergeant Berry rose to the bait and began railroading the small group, with particular venom aimed at Hewson. Naturally the lads all adopted an air of injured innocence and, almost to a man, protested that they hadn't mentioned anyone's names. They were just chatting about things they had heard. Almost everyone present, including other NCOs, joined in the chorus of 'Give it a miss, Sergeant – we're having our breakfast.'

After this incident it was noticeable that Sergeant Berry seemed to mellow a bit in his attitude towards the lads. Hewson told me that a number of the men in the machine-gun section had rebelled against him in various subtle ways, such that his nervous state was affected to the extent that he would often send other NCOs and privates to check on things that he should have done personally.

A week or so after this incident, Talbot, our poet laureate, was involved in an incident with Hewson which caused him to write some of his best lines. At about 0200 hrs on one very cold morning in December, I was on duty in our command bunker when there was a significant explosion in the machine-gun area, which was below us to our right. When I phoned the section Hewson answered and said that they were investigating the incident. I immediately woke our Sergeant Jones and everyone was stood to. No one got any sleep that night and we were all glad to see daylight. The phones were ringing throughout the night as the different companies checked in to find out what was happening. All we could tell them was that either a grenade or a mine had gone off – reason not known.

Next morning at breakfast, I managed to get hold of Hewson and in hushed tones he told me the true story. At about 0145 hrs he had come off stag and had woken Talbot to do the next turn. Hewson had barely got his head down when Talbot came into the bunker and told him he thought someone was on the wire. Now to be woken up roughly from a blessed sleep is not exactly guaranteed to make you feel highly delighted, so it was a rather grumpy Hewson who followed his mate outside. It was true that the enemy did on occasions try to sneak through the wire defences, but equally, noises were often made by animals such as deer getting caught up. There was one animal which they called a mountain lion which, when caught, would hiss and snarl in a most eerie way. Although the Koreans called it a lion, it was in reality some kind of wild cat. It was also true that as night fell, bushes and trees could turn into people until you got used to the night watches. On this particular night, however, Hewson was in no mood to speculate, so he pulled a grenade and slung it, with the words, 'Share that amongst you!' As described, this act set telephones ringing all down the line, but when questioned Hewson and Talbot stuck to their story that someone had trodden on a mine or had thrown a grenade. I think few people believed them but only a couple of select people knew the true story.

It was very true that guard duty could be a bit nerve-racking and there was one case later in the year when a new officer thought fireflies were tracer rounds, and made the mistake of 'standing to' his platoon. This resulted in the platoon being nicknamed 'the firefly platoon'. Experience taught us to differentiate between the real and imaginary enemy, but there was no doubt that in the long night watches, nerves would be on edge and deciphering the many sights and sounds was not always easy.

Following the grenade incident, Talbot came up with one of his best poems, which I now quote below.

On guard

When I stand on guard outside our OP
A few thousand Chinese I often see,
They creep down the valley so silently,
Two thousand Chinkies all after me.
I cock my Bren and stand alert,
Then I wipe my brow with the cuff of my shirt.
They are close enough now so I fire a burst,
Some die instantly, some suffer first.

By now I'm surrounded,
My legs just sag.
Then Rogerson wakes me
'Come on – you're on stag!'

Incidents like the one quoted were good light entertainment, which helped to break what was sometimes a rather monotonous routine, caused by static warfare. Living in bunkers and trenches with all the long hours of watching and waiting, was very tiring and a great strain on the nerves.

The fetching and carrying of supplies, the wiring and patrol work were often carried out in cold, biting winds or pouring rain, and as the winter advanced the fatigue was clearly etched on the faces of all the men. It was the relentlessness of the situation which was hard to deal with as the days turned into weeks and the weeks into months. Seven days a week, 18- or even 24-hour days were the norm, with no hope of relief. Men like Hewson were good men to have around, although a little undisciplined as many Liverpudlians are (they will do anything for you by request, but not by order) and he was very reliable and loyal to his mates.

On a number of occasions he had picked me up in his jeep after I had been out mending broken lines and had dropped me at the bottom of Pioneer Hill. Although the lines were across country, as soon as they were mended we would make our way to the nearest dust track road, which not only made walking easier but also offered the chance of a lift. Hewson, being the character he was, had no compunction about making our officer wait if he saw me on the road making my way back to what had become home. His philosophy was that it was more important to look after the lads doing the hard bit, than the upper echelons. As he put it, 'You have to look after the important people.'

There was one incident, however, when a lift from Hewson was of doubtful merit. I heard his brakes squeal as he pulled up and when I turned around I was surprised to see he had Captain Swift with him. The Captain was a popular officer because he could maintain discipline without recourse to any rigid army-type discipline. Strict but fair, he could be one of the lads, yet could be relied on to lead his men without fear or favour. Later in the year I became quite friendly with him when he trained the company and battalion boxing teams, of which I became a part. He even boxed with and against some privates, which is a rare thing for an officer to do.

Ever grateful for a lift, I jumped into the back of the jeep and in no time at all we were speeding along at some 30–40mph. Near the front line, vehicles were not allowed to do more than about 40mph maximum, because if they did the dust kicked up could be seen by the enemy who would shell the area in the hope of hitting something or someone. As we drove along, Captain Swift, in his quiet voice, began to goad Hewson into driving faster by making aggravating comments such as, 'I thought you were a fast driver, Hewson.'

'I am a fast driver,' protested Hewson, 'but if I do drive fast in this area, I will probably get charged if I get caught.'

'Who will the charge be sent to?' said our wily Captain.

'You sir,' said Hewson.

'Precisely,' said Swift.

As he uttered these words I felt myself being pushed back in my seat as Hewson's foot powered down on the accelerator. Bushes and trees flashed by as we sped ever faster along the dusty mountain roads, all the while Captain Swift egging him on with comments such as, 'I suppose you could drive quickly if you really tried. What do you think, Williams?'

What did I think? I was sitting in the back of this bouncing vehicle, beginning to wonder that perhaps the Chinese weren't the most dangerous people around. As we pulled up at the bottom of Pioneer Hill, Captain Swift made a remark to the effect that it was a good job they had spotted me. I replied that I wouldn't be offended if the next time they saw me they didn't bother to stop, at which they drove away, grinning broadly.

It's a strange phenomenon that when people are in a war situation, where they should be doing everything they can to avoid injury or even death, they often get into a frame of mind which causes them to take unnecessary risks.

Of course, Hewson wasn't the only driver who could make life exciting for his customers. Ivor Davies, one of the lads in our intake at Brecon, was also a star turn in a jeep.

Ivor it was who, during an inter-platoon football match, had showed our drill Sergeant that though the Sergeant was an expert on the parade ground, Ivor was equally expert on the football pitch, and had landed the Sergeant in the mud just to prove it.

Ivor's party piece was to waltz his jeep round steep mountain-road bends using his handbrake. I had been with him a few times so I was aware of this tricky manoeuvre, but on one occasion when he was giving me a lift he picked up a couple of unsuspecting customers. Before the journey was finished I think they were seriously considering whether to stick it out or jump for safety before he stopped.

One thing for sure in Korea was that although the money was poor, the excitement at times was almost unbearably good.

On a more serious note, some time later Hewson had one very lucky escape when his vehicle was hit by a shell which killed the Korean porter who was with him, and wounded one of his mates. As if that wasn't enough, he then had another incident where shrapnel came through his windscreen. Ever the optimist, whenever I met him he was ready for a laugh and a joke – a good man to have around.

Chapter 11

Christmas at the Front

As Christmas 1951 drew near, our thoughts quite naturally turned to home. Whatever the weather back in the UK we knew our Christmas would be a white one. With each passing day the temperatures dropped and the ground froze even harder. Digging became so difficult that the Assault Pioneers were called on more and more to carry out controlled blasting in order to get down to softer earth. Unfortunately, the platoon had limited amounts of cordite and gun cotton to do this work, sometimes leading to a bit of leg pulling which didn't go down too well with the lads, because given the resources they could blow anything up.

This situation came to a head when one of the C Company officers overdid the joking to the extent that several of the lads formed a deputation to Lieutenant Mennell with a view to getting extra supplies in order to show C Company that they really could make big bangs and big holes. Lieutenant Mennell was not averse to a good joke so he readily agreed to the requests made. As would be expected, Hewson was to the forefront of this deputation and before the lads set off on this particular morning he said to me, 'Watch the top of C Company hill at 1100 hours today. We're going to ring the hill to make a slit trench, but we're going to blast it all at one go.' Clever stuff!

This performance was not to be missed, so just before the appointed hour I went outside our bunker to watch this interesting spectacle. Sure enough at 1100 hrs a whistle sounded and there was an almighty bang as if a huge bomb had gone off, followed by smoke and showers of earth and rocks flying into the air, right around the top of C Company hill. This was followed by the sight of figures running in all directions as the earth rained down.

As would be expected, our phone rang a few minutes later and when I answered an irate C Company Commander wanted to speak to Lieutenant Mennell. The Lieutenant had to stifle his laughter as he picked up the phone, but in a serious tone he carefully explained that because they had dropped behind with the blasting programme he had told his lads to speed things up. He said that he hoped that the lads had carried out the necessary warning procedures (which they had) but he would check with them when they returned to base.

When the lads did get back he called them together and gave them a mock dressing down. 'You stupid boys,' he said, 'you shouldn't have frightened C Company like that!'

'Sorry sir,' came the reply, as everyone burst out laughing.

'That will teach the buggers to complain,' observed Mennell. 'Well done, lads.'

Our cook made Christmas something to remember by laying on a slap-up meal. Food was in plentiful supply, so it was double chicken and turkey legs all round. However, no one could have anticipated the surreal picture that met our eyes on Christmas Day. Right in the middle of no-man's land was a huge Christmas tree, decorated with presents. Because the Assault Pioneers were nearest to this strange gift, and because they were the people to check for booby traps, we got first choice of everything on the tree.

When the lads returned with the items they had collected, we all had a good laugh as we selected what we wanted. There were gifts including printed handkerchiefs embellished with slogans such as 'Demand peace and stop war', and safe-conduct passes which were supposed to help you give yourself up to the Chinese. I carried mine in my top pocket and would always get a laugh by showing it to the lads. There was also an attractive little lapel badge with an enamelled dove on it, engraved with the same words as on the handkerchiefs, which I still have as a keepsake.

Once word got round that the lads in the Assault Pioneers had removed the presents from the Chinese Christmas tree, we had a deluge of officers and other personnel arriving, all hoping to acquire a few pieces. Although very acceptable, these gifts from the Chinese did nothing to diminish our war effort. In fact, I think the reverse was the case. I also collected a variety of pamphlets which our propaganda people dropped from aircraft onto the Chinese positions – I donated them to the Liverpool Museum in 1954, when they put on a Korean War exhibition. Not infrequently, when the wind was in the wrong direction, the leaflets would drift back over us. Because the Russians were backing China in this conflict, the leaflets often depicted a mask of the smiling face of Stalin, behind which was a scowling face, backed by lines of Red soldiers.

Thankfully, the Christmas tree was not booby-trapped and with festivities over we soon headed into the very coldest part of the winter. In the sub-zero temperatures we were more than glad to have our fur-lined parka coats, and it was said that they cost some £10, which in the 1950s was more than a tradesman's weekly wage. In fact, when one got lost there was a court of inquiry.

Food and warmth were priorities under such conditions and I had never realized before how easy it would be to go to sleep and die of exposure. Standing guard in the freezing cold I would often feel my legs sag as I momentarily went to sleep standing up. A great pick-me-up on these long night watches was a specially designed can of meat which had a tube through the centre with a fuse which could be lit. Once ignited the fuse would heat up the can in a few minutes and you could eat a couple of burger-type meat balls. I think the design was American, but I have never seen a similar arrangement before or since. With the urge and need to eat to keep warm almost everyone put a stone on in weight during the winter, but it would soon be lost when the summer arrived.

To give an idea of how cold it was in that location, I will quote the case of the broken telephone line to the standing patrol. On this particular occasion, it broke down about two in the morning. Corporal C, Domonic and I set off to find the break and mend it. Once located, the fault would, under normal conditions, have taken three or four minutes to repair, which was done by paring the broken ends, tying them together and then applying some insulation tape around the join. With temperatures around -35^0 we found that about twenty seconds after taking our gloves off, our hands were so cold the wire had to be dropped and one of the others would continue the task, whilst the first man stuck his hands inside his parka under his armpits. Working with a shaded torch didn't help and it took us some twenty minutes to carry out this rudimentary task. At times, we could hardly stop ourselves laughing, such were our feeble attempts at this normally simple operation. To add insult to injury, when we returned to base we were asked what had taken us so long!

On a lighter note, another incident occurred which also helps to illustrate just how cold it was during the winter months. It involved a discussion on what was the best way to go to the toilet in the middle of the night. Our number one storyteller, Sergeant Francis, described his infallible system, as he called it. He said that when he had a night-time urge to go he would, as many of the lads did, wrap a blanket around himself but, instead of going to one of our hillside latrines, he would make for a steep part of the bracken-covered hillside. He would then drop his trousers and do his 'whoopsie', after which he said he would wait three minutes before kicking the offending frozen matter down the hill. Everyone was doubled up at this description, but the laughter reached a crescendo when one of the lads remarked, 'That's not a first, Sergeant!' What made this crude description so funny was that the severe temperatures made it possible. Necessity is often the mother of invention.

Whilst on this slightly unsavoury subject, Sergeant Francis told the tale of how he nearly wrecked a Queen's Parade in Cardiff. At the time he was the Sergeant in charge of the Assault Pioneers and, as such, was the only man in the Battalion to be allowed to wear a beard. The Pioneers on this occasion were leading the parade, when Sergeant Francis spotted a little terrier dog trying to do his daily dozen in the gutter. The dog was trying that hard that its legs were quivering and so out of the corner of his mouth he said, 'Corporal, fall out and squeeze that dog's head.' He only meant the Corporal to hear him, but the comment carried on through the platoon itself and such was the suppressed laughter they all lost their step. Later, when the CO called him to account, he silver-tongued his way out of the situation by suggesting that it looked as if there was a possible security scare and he had told his men to prepare to break ranks – a likely story, but it sufficed. He could hardly admit the incident was due to a little terrier, straight off of the label of a 'His Master's Voice' record.

Although Sergeant Francis was ever ready to see the funny side of things, he was a very intelligent and knowledgeable soldier who could get the best out of the lads without resorting to barrack-room discipline. Much liked and highly regarded, it was a pleasure to serve under his command.

Generally speaking the food we had was good but when, for various reasons, we had to switch to combat rations, there were sometimes a few shortages. On one occasion Francis said to me, 'Get your notepad ready. I'm going to see the Yanks or Canadians. We need some extra tea, eggs and sugar.'

Off he went in a jeep and an hour later he was back with a crate of tinned milk. I ask you – what good was a crate of milk? 'Now,' he said to me, 'this is how to change one not very useful crate of tinned milk into useful commodities.' With that he asked me to telephone C Company's Sergeant Major.

After the usual pleasantries and enquiries concerning their families, and so forth, he put the relevant question. 'Have you got a bit of tea you can spare us, for some quality tinned milk?' Of course they had, came the reply. 'Now Nev,' he said, 'make sure you write down what I tell you in the correct order. Tinned milk for tea, C Company.' Next he had me telephone B Company's Colour Sergeant and, using the same technique, he promised to swap some tinned milk and a little bit of tea for some eggs. He immediately telephoned A Company and swapped tinned milk and a few eggs for sugar. The exercise completed, he took my list and, visiting each site in the correct order, he was able to get us the promised tea, eggs and sugar. Survival techniques of this type are not in any official army training manuals but, without doubt, it's men like Francis who overcome such problems and help to win wars. Food is always of the essence and the colder it is the more you need. Looking back, I can hardly believe how much some men ate when they had been out working in the cold. I remember watching one of our lads eat twelve slices of thick bread with his mess tin full of hot food. Under normal circumstances most men couldn't do that even it they wanted to.

Chapter 12

Operation DISAPPEAR, Comforts and Comradeship

The war in Korea at this time had developed into static warfare, with each side well dug in and surrounded by barbed wire, so that the main contact with the enemy was by shelling and patrol work.

During a period after Christmas it was decided at high level that our Battalion would carry out an operation called DISAPPEAR. The idea was that for two weeks, all movement on the hills we occupied would be restricted to such an extent that our positions would appear to be abandoned. Everyone had to keep well down in the trenches and movement was only allowed on the reverse side of the hills. There was to be no lighting of fires and we had to live on one box of C7 combat rations each day. The hope was that the Chinese would be tempted to probe our positions, thus giving us a chance to take prisoners.

Under the freezing conditions, this exercise was anything but popular, but ours was not to reason why! This fortnight of creeping about seemed interminably long, but eventually ended much to our delight. Although the idea seemed to be reasonable, as far as I could ascertain it was a failure and achieved nothing.

Because the Assault Pioneers were the most forward platoon in the Battalion, most of the patrols that went out had to pass through our positions and this often gave me the chance to have a chat with friends I had trained with in the UK. This patrol work was very nerve- racking and sometimes resulted in casualties. Going out on one of these patrols the lads would often look cheerful, but at the same time were tense. Returning at daybreak they looked altogether different. Their eyes had a haunted look and their faces were almost skeletal, as they plodded wearily back to their positions. No doubt they were glad still to be alive, but they would undoubtedly be suffering the after-effects of tension, fear, relief and utter weariness. In some cases they would also be weighed down by the unwelcome memory of a comrade being wounded or killed. Anyone who has experienced night patrol duties, or seen the return of a patrol, would understand perfectly why such a term as 'shattered' could also be applied to these men.

Before we were to leave Korea, men of our Battalion would carry out many dangerous patrols, some of which involved hand-to-hand fighting, resulting in serious casualties. During the year we were in Korea men of the Welch Regiment received over thirty commendations for bravery, most of which were gained on patrol work.

On one occasion a National Serviceman called Griffiths stopped to have a chat with me when returning from a night out. He said that they had managed to get a couple of prisoners, but on the way back their patrol had been 'bumped' and one of our lads had been wounded, which so incensed the others that they shot the prisoners. Griffiths had been in the same company as me during training and I had no reason to disbelieve him, but nothing official was ever said or done. Wars are not fought to the Marquis of Queensbury Rules and what is acceptable or not acceptable on paper is often not recognized in combat.

As winter progressed we got settled in and I trained a number of lads in elementary phone and wireless procedures so that they could sometimes cover for me when I was on other duties. There was never a shortage of volunteers for this work, but it did occasionally lead to slight misunderstandings. One private called Christie was very keen to have a go at signaller work and I soon had him performing the basics, but when it came to a time check he didn't always get it right. To improve the situation I suggested that when he was on guard one night he should radio me using one of the belt-type, short-range radios and I would give him a check as it should be done.

The night when he was doing his guard duty in the machine-gun section, which was on a low hill to our right, he called me up and asked for a time check. In measured tones I slowly answered his call using the standard procedure. 'When I say time, the time will be zero 1 zero 8, how, roger, sugars [i.e. hours].' I then began the countdown which went: 'Ten, nine, eight, seven, six, five, four, three, two, one. The time is now zero 1 zero 8, how, roger, sugar.' In other words, eight minutes past 0100 hrs. To my surprise, back came the reply in a Chinese-type voice, 'Me no understand, please give in English.'

Almost immediately the battalion control station came on air telling all users to get off the air and close down. The battalion intercept station had thought it really was a Chinese listening station trying to tune in to us. I never took the trouble to enlighten them at our HQ as to what the situation really was, because I do not think they would have been particularly pleased if I had. Of course Christie was absolutely amazed at the reaction caused by his Chinese impersonation but, as I explained to him at breakfast the next day, secure wireless procedures are essential on active service. Being a Liverpudlian, Christie thought it was a good laugh, which in retrospect it probably was.

Personal experience is a great teacher, but sometimes the outcome can be a bit painful, as it was when our third man, Domonic, joined us and went out to mend his first broken line. A chubby, cheerful, cockney lad, he was good to have around and soon after joining us he volunteered to trace one of our broken lines to our F Echelon supply base. A pretty straightforward job, we thought, as did Domonic. He cheerfully set off and in due course our phone rang, the caller being Domonic, reporting that he had found the break and that it would be mended within a few minutes. Some ten minutes later our officer came in to enquire if he could get through to our F Echelon. I confidently reported that the line should now be mended but when I rang, the handle on our phone generator moved stiffly which meant that the current was still going to earth. After about five minutes I rang again and the call went through as normal. Neither Corporal C nor I thought much more about the situation, but when Domonic returned about an hour later he was highly agitated, jumping up and down, as they say, and threatening blue murder – not that he could have carried out his threats.

As the story unfolded it transpired that when he had traced the broken ends of the telephone cables, they were so chewed up (probably a tank or similar) he had found that he had to scrounge some extra cable to make up for the missing piece, and when I had rung in he was in the process of mending the line. Unfortunately, he had put the bared ends of the wire in his teeth whilst he paired the adjoining piece of wire. Wet teeth and telephone wires make an ideal path for electric current and when I had rung he must have had sparks flying out of his ears. Although the generating battery was only 4 volts, turning the handle vigorously could create a fair old amperage. When he told us what had happened everyone was convulsed with laughter with thoughts of Domonic doing a Highland fling and looking like a 'sparkler' on bonfire night. The practice of gripping wires in the mouth was a common one, but not by the non-insulated portion. Domonic had learned a valuable lesson which he would never forget and it must be said that there's nothing like hands-on (or in this case teeth) experience. Ouch!

Living in a hole in the ground is not the best way to spend a sub-zero winter, but by January we had made many welcome additions to our bunkers. Not only was the roof logged, but gradually we lined the walls, and because our command bunker was so large, I took it upon myself to put in lots of wooden piers to make sure that there was no danger of collapse. As previously described, pickets and machine-gun belts made excellent beds, and chairs and tables were soon constructed out of surplus wooden boxes. At night the bunker was lit by a variety of methods, including candles – lights made from old tins which had a wick-fed tube inserted into paraffin or petrol – and quite often we would use old wireless batteries which were no longer fit for purpose, but when connected in series had enough power to light various bulbs. Similarly, our home-made, ex-ammunition box stoves gave out plenty of light and heat, provided there was a plentiful supply of wood, and the petrol-fed space heaters were useful except when they overheated and vaporized. However, a number of people got burned by these badly designed contraptions, so they were not the most favoured piece of issue equipment.

When it came to clothes washing the Korean porters were a great help. For a few cigarettes, or similar enticement, they would often do the laundry for us, sometimes boiling the articles in large cast-iron pots or beating them on a rock in the nearby river. Even in winter the sun was often quite warm by midday, which helped the drying process, but if not the clothes would be hung near a fire. In the case of socks, I used to change mine every day. I hung the freshly washed ones on my pack, as did many of the lads, so that they would dry as we went about our duties. Interestingly, the Koreans could wash and smooth shirts as if they had been ironed and they did this by careful movements of the hands across the fabric just before the clothes were fully dry. As a young lad I had seen my grandmother do the same thing so no doubt this old skill went way back and was very effective.

When watching the telephone exchange all night I would often play patience or read to pass the time and, being keen on art, I would often draw. The lads always liked cartoon-type sketches so I would produce something which could be hung in their bunkers.

As already mentioned, during our early days in Korea I had been given a small copy of the biblical story relating to 'The Sermon on the Mount', and the more I read this timeless work the more I realized the eternal truths it contained. In this short work there is a God-given and never-ending message to all mankind which can be called on to provide insight into all manner of human affairs. The guidance I found in this amazing passage has been a constant blessing throughout my life and I would recommend it to all who would like to find an anchor in faith.

To this end our battalion padre would visit each company every Sunday and perform a short service. Being a practising Christian I enjoyed these services and I would often nip round our platoon to dig out some of the lads who were half-hearted about their attendance. Their grumbles when I did this were without any real conviction and I think it would be true to say that everyone appreciated the services. There is nothing like imminent danger to make one aware of one's mortality. Many times I had quite in-depth conversations with my mates on serious subjects which would have been difficult to engender in normal life. However, when skies were blue and things were quiet it was difficult to believe that only three quarters of a mile away Chinese soldiers were dug in and, if required, would have no compunction about killing us if the chance arose. If there was a danger of us being lulled into a sense of false security it would often be broken by the news that one of our mates had been wounded or, worse, killed.

I remember hearing about a young lad called Rowe who was killed in a jeep by a stray shell, which was very sad. When we were in the barracks in Colchester he was in the next bed to me, and a more inoffensive and genuine lad you couldn't wish to meet. Although not cut out to be an infantryman, he got stuck into whatever was asked of him and made the best of it. In Korea he had eventually found a niche in the mechanical transport section. What a slender thread life hangs from. Another day, another time, another place and he might have lived to tell the tale. What must his parents have thought and felt?

On another occasion, I was out on a line near A Company when I espied two stretcher-bearers bringing a wounded comrade down the hill. It turned out to be none other than my old mate N, the lad I had had to scrub when we first arrived at Brecon training camp. A real character, we had remained firm friends during training and had done many a patrol out on the battle training area in Norfolk. As the stretcher-bearers reached me, they stopped while I had a brief chat with my friend who had been shot in the ankle. He was laughing all over his face as he informed me that he was being taken to Kuree, which was a little island off the coast of mainland Japan where soldiers could be treated and given rest and recuperation. In his best sergeant major voice, he imitated, 'Carry on, soldier!' and as they carried him away I could hear him singing, 'Kuree, here I come'. A great little character, he was full of fun. I remember being on a bus with him in Colchester when the conductor jokingly passed some remark about his hat, to which N immediately replied in a sergeant major's voice, 'Stand still, you dozy individual.' He then proceeded to do a mock inspection of the bus conductor. 'Belt too slack, dirty buttons, tie not lined up. Shoes not polished.' The conductor played his part and the bus rocked with laughter, such was the infectious humour of this 'never-say-die' little character.

A couple of months after seeing him on the stretcher, I bumped into him back on A Company hill. Cocky as ever he said, 'I'm fit enough to be shot at again, so here I am! It was OK on Kuree,' he said, 'but I'm glad to be back with the lads – back at the sharp end.' It may seem strange that this young soldier should prefer the battle zone to a reserve position, but I knew what he meant. Amongst tried and trusted comrades there develops a bond which is hard to rationalize.

Chapter 13

Prisoners and a Prelude to Spring

As already mentioned, one or our top priorities with regard to communication was to make sure that our line to the Standing Patrol was maintained, so that they could always contact us or HQ. Imagine my surprise one bright sunny morning when the phone rang and a voice asked, 'Is there a Korean patrol going out through our positions today?' The question was definitely odd and not one I had ever been asked before. Korean ROK soldiers were not near us and certainly never came through our positions. There was definitely something fishy about this enquiry. I was the only NCO on site that day so I immediately rang HQ and asked the obvious question. The answer was a very positive 'no'. These soldiers, whoever they were, could only be the enemy. They were to be stopped and brought in for questioning.

I quickly phoned the NCO at the standing patrol and told him to disarm the so-called ROK soldiers and we would be along as soon as possible to take them back to HQ. I had no trouble rounding up half a dozen volunteers to go with me and within a few minutes we ready and on our way. I had told each of the lads to take a fully loaded rifle and a couple of grenades. If there was any resistance they were to shoot anyone who looked like firing on us. We were going into a very unusual situation so discipline and a positive attitude were essential. Who were these intruders and why were they on our side of the wire?

Trotting in single file, we reached the standing patrol in about ten minutes or so, but to my consternation, when we arrived, the Korean soldiers had not been relieved of their weaponry and were having a heated discussion with the patrol. This was definitely not a healthy situation. When the North Koreans saw us they became very agitated and I could see by their expressions that they were in two minds what to do. The Corporal in charge of the Standing Patrol had a light machine gun trained on the unwelcome visitors, but since the situation was highly volatile there was only one thing for it. 'When I give the order,' I told my lads, 'cock your rifles and move in to disarm them. I will take the leader. Shoot anyone who tries to start anything.' I then told the Corporal on the light machine gun, 'If anyone causes a problem as we move in, shoot the leader.'

The North Korean officer glared at me as I pointed my rifle at him and removed the grenades from his belt. I could see by the look in his eyes he was in two minds what to do, but the odds were stacked against these unfortunates, so that although they babbled away in pigeon English, they offered no real resistance. Once disarmed I instructed the lads to make the prisoners put their hands on their heads and get into single file, with one of them just behind and to the side of each prisoner. In this formation we marched them down the dusty road back to our HQ which was about one and a half miles away. Every now and then one of the prisoners would try to go slower or lower their hands, but I told the lads to operate the bolt on their rifle when this happened and to give the prisoner a prod – if they did make a run for it, I ordered the lads to shoot them in the legs. The prisoners knew the score and when we arrived at HQ we handed them over to one of the sergeants who told us they would be sent further down the line for questioning. One thing was for sure, they would take no further part in the war.

As we strolled back to our own positions we were much given to discussing the day's events. I don't think any of us were too impressed with the way the Standing Patrol had dealt with the situation. By allowing the enemy to retain their weapons, there might have been a gun battle and the North Koreans could have escaped. As it was, it was a case of all's well that ends well.

When we got back to our hill, everyone wanted to know the details of the sortie, but we were all puzzled to know how a North Korean patrol could end up on our side of the wire in broad daylight, apparently lost. When I enquired about the prisoners some time later, I was told that they had been sent out on what was almost certainly a suicide patrol, having committed some kind of misdemeanour, and that they gave our intelligence people some useful information. As far as I could asceetain, these prisoners were the only ones taken by our Battalion.

As winter began to give way to spring, life returned to the undergrowth and bushes. Being tinder dry, it was easy for some of the bushes to catch fire and on one occasion we were treated to a real bush fire which started in the Chinese positions and gradually swept down the Samichon Valley towards our positions. As it crept nearer we realized it wasn't just an interesting sight but a possible danger to our emplacement, so everyone had to set to with shovels and axes to stop its spread. Fortunately, it burned itself out when only about a third of the way up the hill, but on reflection we wondered whether the Chinese had started it deliberately, for the wind was certainly blowing in our direction.

We had several officers in charge during the four months we were on Pioneer Hill, and the last but one, Lieutenant Mennell, was a most likeable and lively character. I think the CO rated him a good officer and on several occasions invited him to HQ for dinner. This never happened to Major Parry whilst he was in charge of Support Company. I once heard him complaining to Mennell that the CO should go through him to offer such rather privileged days out. I suspected that the CO had deliberately bypassed Major Parry because he was not very impressed by his style and performance.

Lieutenant Mennell did a fare amount of patrol work, which was very taxing, but he made light of it and on one occasion I put him through from the Standing Patrol to give a report on his night's works. The conversation would normally be rather serious, but this time the Lieutenant, being the light-hearted spirit he was, couldn't help making a joke out of the report.

Corporal C and I could listen to any conversations which came through our exchange, so quite naturally we were more than interested in this one. Mennell said that he had come across a very strange situation. He told the CO that he had crept very near to the enemy positions and when within hearing distance, they detected a dull thumping noise. In order to find out what it was they crept even closer. 'What was the noise?' enquired the CO, who was as curious as we were. Then came the crunch line. Mennell said that they had found out that nearly all the Chinese had one wooden leg. Few people would have tried to put over on the CO like that, but he obviously enjoyed the Lieutenant's humour and roared with laughter.

Sad to say, later in the year, this likeable blithe spirit of a man got shot up and when I returned to the UK he was at Maindy Barracks, Cardiff. Along with one of our sergeants, he came out to meet us when we were picked up and delivered to the barracks by truck. Gaunt and pale, he had obviously suffered much and was only a shadow of the man I had known in Korea. He had truly paid the price of war. I never saw him again, but often thought about him.

A month or so before we left Pioneer Hill to go into reserve, Lieutenant Mennell left us and was replaced by Lieutenant Brindlecombe. A firm disciplinarian, he was not at all welcome at first, as the lads had heard he was a bit of a hard man. First impressions tended to confirm this because on his arrival he had everyone brushing out the trenches to barrack-room standards. To some degree this was quite normal, but the officers didn't generally do a daily inspection.

As a Regimental Signaller I was always at the point of contact between the officers and the troops. The officers' bunker was next to the command bunker and since all the wireless and phone services were in there, as a signaller you were always privileged to know what was going on. Under active service conditions your daily contact with the officers allowed a much more friendly and relaxed relationship than would be possible whilst in barracks.

On his first night in charge, Lieutenant Brindlecombe asked the cook to bring him some chicken sandwiches, which no doubt he enjoyed, but the lads on guard were not impressed. Standing half the night in freezing conditions was no joke, especially when the officer in charge comes to inspect you whilst eating a sandwich. This style of inspection generated a fair amount of animosity and grumbles. After a couple of days Lieutenant Brindlecombe came into the bunker one night and got quite chatty. He suddenly said to me, 'How do you think I'm doing, Williams?' I looked hard at him and could see he really did want to know. Under the hard exterior was a very keen, decent man, who had come up the hard way in that he had been granted his commission after coming up through the ranks. This seemed to have made him a bit overzealous, which is often the case.

'Well sir,' I replied, tongue in cheek, 'these lads are a very good bunch who really know their job, so I know you can trust them, but they were a bit put out when they saw that tray of sandwiches go into the bunker last night, especially when they didn't get a look in.'

He seemed to take my remarks in good part and the next night, much to everyone's surprise, he had sandwiches brought up, but this time he had them dished out to the guards. Needless to say, the lads very quickly reassessed the new boss and decided he wasn't such a bad sort after all.

Lieutenant Brindlecombe quickly settled in to the Assault Pioneer Platoon and I think he quite liked the work, which was a change from the machine-gun section from whence he'd come. He was a quick learner and I found him a good, reliable officer to work for. He was certainly more able than our Major Parry, who had now departed to become a liaison officer. Since the Major had left our position, we only saw him once after that, when he turned up quite unexpectedly. I suppose it could have been a sort of farewell visit but, whatever his reasons, he didn't stay long in the command bunker when he saw me priming grenades. He arrived with a flourish and departed rather quickly, but not before he had seen the cartoon of himself pinned on one of the bunker uprights, the caricature depicting him with a parrot-like nose, and the caption reading 'Pecker Parry', which was his nickname amongst the lads. When he saw it he scowled, but surprisingly didn't take it down or directly refer to it. In his better moments I think he was not a bad officer, but I always felt he was not really suited to the infantry. A rather delicate-looking man, probably well into his forties, and not very fit, Korea was not exactly the sort of place he would be expected to enjoy. We were only National Servicemen, drafted in without any choice, but since he was a regular – the Army was his choice of career – I think most of the lads thought he ought to have been more able and enthusiastic. His nervous and rather snappy disposition did not go down well and everyone was glad to see him go. Of course, looking back, I can now see how difficult a place like Korea would be for any middle-aged man.

In all fairness, I couldn't judge the Major too harshly, because he was Major Parry MC, so he must have seen action before Korea, and who knows what effect that might have had on him.

In war, and in life in general, it is not always what we do that causes stress, but sometimes what we see or hear. This was brought sharply into focus for me years later when as a Safety Officer I had to investigate serious accidents. In one case, a tradesman was crushed to death by a heavy casting which toppled and trapped him, severing an artery, so that he was dead within seconds. It turned out it was his own error which caused the accident, but the crane driver involved was so traumatized by witnessing the accident he couldn't face driving the overhead crane again. He told me every time he looked down he could envisage this awful occurrence happening again.

Although we were miles from civilization, there was no real shortage of alcoholic drink. Whilst in the line we were paid in NAAFI baffs, which could be used to order such things as chocolates, cigarettes and beer. We were also given a rum ration so it was no surprise that from time to time some of the lads got a bit tipsy. Corporal C, being a regular, was rather prone to overdo the drinking aspect and on one particular night he went to see one of his mates who also liked a tipple. He took with him some saved-up rum ration, so we guessed they were going to have a good session. When he returned about 2200 hrs, I was having a chat with Sergeant Jones, Domonic and one or two others, but when Corporal C came into the bunker the conversation stopped dead. He lurched from side to side and it was obvious he was well and truly plastered. Oblivious to us he staggered to his picket bed and fell into it. Everyone grinned and we knew that he wouldn't be doing his stint on the phone and wireless sets. Strangely enough, before he fell into bed he took his boots off, which was not the normal drill when turning in, since we always slept with our boots on. He had hardly got into bed when he more or less fell out again and to our amazement began to urinate in one of his boots. I had heard of this being done by one or two corporals whilst in barracks, but never in their own boots. Having relieved himself, he carefully put his boot down, got into bed and promptly fell into a deep sleep. Domonic and I knew we would have to do his stag that night, but everyone wondered what Corporal C's reaction would be when eventually he came round.

By stand-to the next morning, word had got round about Corporal C's boot, so that when it was time for him to emerge from his slumbers, a small select band of comrades had assembled to witness the final part of this comedy. Rather bleary eyed, our morning-after Corporal eventually opened his bloodshot eyes and gazed in a rather mystified way at the assembled group. Bending down as he slid out of bed, he picked up his waterlogged boot. Suddenly he was wide awake.

'What dirty bugger did this?' he exploded.

'Sorry,' I said, 'but who's holding the boot?'

At this his face took on a look of incredulity. 'I haven't! I didn't! I couldn't! Oh, bloody hell!'

The main act over, the onlookers sidled away, everyone grinning widely as they did so. As they left the bunker Corporal C could be heard pleading, 'Don't tell the lads.' As if they would!

By dinner time half the Battalion had heard the news and since it was Corporal C's turn to man the telephone exchange he was able to receive the messages of condolence first hand. The phone would ring. 'Sorry about your accident, pal, but my auntie in Cardiff has a spare left boot if you're interested.'

Someone else would ring. 'Is it true the eyeholes on your boots turned green?' Then another solicitous mate rang. 'The Chinese were lucky they didn't attack last night. If you had thrown that boot at them that would've been the end of the Korean War!'

Eventually Corporal C had had enough and made himself scarce for the rest of the day. Sympathy is OK, but you can only stand so much of it. Of course, looking at this incident from a positive point of view, Corporal C had caused half the Battalion to smile that day, and it was noticeable thereafter that he did modify his drinking habits.

Whilst drink in the form of bottled beer was always available to the lads in the front line, it was not, in my experience, any kind of a real problem. However, there were a few rather comical incidents because of it. I think it was true to say that by and large the regulars were far more likely to imbibe rather more so than the National Servicemen, this being particularly true of sergeants, especially when they got together. One of the funniest stories recounted to me was that told by Sergeant Smith of D Company.

Smithy had been my small-arms and drill instructor whilst in the UK and a better man at his job you couldn't wish to meet. He was a full Corporal in those days but got made up to Sergeant when we went to Korea. Whilst out on a telephone line one day I bumped into him and after a chat about things in general, he told me the following story.

Smithy had done quite a few patrols, but on the particular night in question they had returned back to base in the early hours. He said they were so wound up that they couldn't sleep so they decided to crack open a few bottles. A sergeant, one of their friends, had joined them, but by the time it was time to go the Sergeant friend was so inebriated, Smithy had to support him back to his bunker. It was raining hard and very muddy, so it was with great difficulty that they staggered along. The Sergeant was well away with the fairies and, as such, decided he was a bat. In site of the pleadings of his mates he insisted on climbing up onto a branch of a tree. From there he spread out his poncho wings exclaiming, 'I can fly!'

'You know what,' said Smithy, 'he couldn't fly.'

Fortunately he was unhurt but ended up soaking wet and filthy, much to the amusement of Sergeant Smith and the others helping him.

Under the conditions we were enduring, incidents like these were bound to happen occasionally, but there is no doubt that they provided some light relief. However, living in the open in harsh Korean winters was undoubtedly a grinding-down process. Faces became increasingly gaunt and the lack of sleep made night duties progressively difficult. During one spell I went nearly three days without sleep, and when I did manage to get my head down I can remember the utter exhaustion and light headedness as I fell into a deep, dreamless sleep.

However, as we neared the end of February, life began to creep back into the undergrowth and the word 'reserve' began to enter the conversations. No one was quite sure what the term 'reserve' really meant, but it was generally accepted that it was something to do with getting your head down without going on guard every night.

Chapter 14

Porters and Poetry

During our four-month stay on Pioneer Hill, everyone had been very impressed by the work done by the Korean porters. Honest, resourceful and hardworking we had much to owe to these stalwart characters. I had made very good friends with a number of these men and in particular, Kim and his friend Chan. At one time in the winter the porters had been used to helping out on guard duties. They were not allowed to carry arms but could act as a second man. During this time I had some stand-ins with Chan and had got him to teach me a Number One Korean song. I had heard the porters sing this particular melody which was called 'Ardy Dong' and I liked the sound of it. It took several nights to master the words and Chinese sounding tune but I managed them eventually. After that whenever I sang it I would always get a smile from anyone who listened to my rendition. Sometimes, when I passed a group of Korean porters, digging monsoon ditches or carrying out other useful works, I would burst into song and invariably the group would stop and put their thumbs up. I didn't know what the words meant but here is how it went:

Ardy Dong

Ardy-dong, Ardy Dong Ard Dardee Yo Eo
Ardy-dong Ko Ke dull Nomaganda
Nordul-Pordy Ko Kashin Nanimum
Shimnido r- Morkarso Pall Pyonge Nan Naye.

Chan told me that this was a very popular Korean song which told a story about a man leaving home and crossing the mountains. Later on, when we went into reserve, Lieutenant Brindlecombe formed a battalion choir of which I became a member. When he found out I could sing 'Ardy Dong', he got me to teach the choir. To hear Welsh voices singing in Korean to what sounded like Chinese-style music, must have been very strange indeed.

In due course it was arranged for the choir to give a performance to the officers and men of the Norfolk Regiment. The choir sang a mixture of modern and old choral pieces, but for a finale we were to sing 'Ardy Dong'. Before we could get halfway through our party piece the audience began to laugh – not unexpectedly – and gradually the members began to pick up the vibes, until by the last line both the audience and the choir were in hysterics. As a party piece 'Ardy Dong' had succeeded far better than could have been anticipated, but not exactly as we thought. Even to this day, if I sing the old song it invariably causes amusement.

I have always liked music and poetry, and during the boat journey to Korea, and later on during the long night watches, I memorized quite a few poems and barrack-room ballads. Kipling, Rupert Brooke, Siegfried Sassoon and others, all contributed to my repertoire, plus some poems passed on by some of the regulars. One or two of these old poems were said to be seditious and probably dated back to the First World War, but whatever their origins, the lads liked to hear them. Quite often, if we were doing some digging or wiring, the lads would say to me, 'Give us a few verses, Nev.'

'The Shooting of Dan McGrew' was popular and I know the lads associated themselves with certain verses which struck a chord with them. To quote:

> When you're ever out in the great alone,
> When the night was awful clear
> And the icy mountains hemmed you in
> With a silence you could almost hear.
> Whilst overhead, green, yellow and red,
> The North lights swept in bars
> Then you've a hunch what the music meant
> Hunger, night and the stars.
>
> And hunger not of the belly kind
> That's banished by bacon and beans
> But the gnawing hunger of a lonely heart
> For a home and all it means.

> For a fireside far from the cares that are
> Four walls and a roof above,
> But oh so cram' full of cosy joy
> And crowned with a woman's love.

'Gunga Din' and 'Mad Carew' were two other popular poems which can appeal to ordinary people but which are often mocked by art critics.

My father did four years on the North-West Frontier of India and he said that natives who were water carriers (gunga dins) were absolutely essential in the harsh summer climate. Stanley Holloway's monologues were also popular ('Albert and the Lion', etc.), but like many branches of art, things move on.

Although regimental signallers were attached to various companies and platoons, we were classed as a platoon in our own right. During our training days we had all worked together so that even when we were split up there was a bond between us, such that we always kept in touch. During the mornings and evenings we would open up our 62 wireless sets and report in, each station giving its signal strength grade 1–5. We recorded this information on a chart so that if the signal strength was low to or from a particular company we could still make contact via other companies not so affected.

The open-up and shut-down procedure was usually uneventful, but imagine our surprise when one morning we got a message from someone in the rear of the Division which was sent in US Ops Code. This code was secret, only to be used for very important information. Eagerly, we began to copy the letters down which were meaningless until they were compared against the decode sheet. A letter C might become a J but in some cases a double RR might become an A, and so on. As it happened, in this particular case the voice relaying the message was instantly recognizable by me as that of a Private Lewis. He had been a firm friend of Lamacraft, Jim Sibeon and I during our training days and had often made up the fourth one of our group.

A lively character, Lewis had soon distinguished himself on active service and had been awarded a Mention in Despatches. I think he found this honour slightly embarrassing, especially when some of the lads began to call him MID Lewis. However, shortly after receiving this award he got the wrong side of his company commander and as a result got posted back to a reserve position in Divisional HQ.

So here was Lewis on the line with a whole division listening in to his important message. Slowly we copied the letters down and then began to decode them. As the message unfolded I could hardly believe my eyes. The first word was 'up', followed by 'you', followed by 'from someone in rear Div.' 'Up you, from someone in rear Div.' We had hardly copied the message down when the control station came on the air and told us to shut down. I didn't know how many people might know who was sending this cheeky message, but it was obvious there would be repercussions.

A few days after this incident Lewis arrived back with his mates in the line and when I next met him we had a good laugh about the incident. He told me that he had become number one suspect for this incident, but he had kept his face straight and bluffed it out. As a punishment they had sent him back up to the front line which was what he wanted, but what a risky Brer Rabbit trick to pull.

Later in the year, when I was sent on R & R (Rest and Recuperation), someone behind the scenes thoughtfully arranged for Lewis, Jim Sibeon and Lamacraft to take leave, so that Tokyo had the doubtful privilege of being visited by us all at the same time.

During our stay in Korea the callsigns used over our radios, and also used to halt people when on guard duty, were frequently changed to stop the enemy picking up on them. The words themselves were also chosen such that the Chinese would have difficulty in saying them – or at least that's what we were told. Words such as crucial, able, even Mickey Mouse, were all used, so it was not surprising that on occasions everyone forgot them. This was especially true of the words used to halt someone when on guard. However, British soldiers being that breed of men who are very good at adapting simple solutions to what can be awkward or difficult problems, it wasn't long before a universal password was developed and used when someone forgot the password of the day.

The command 'Halt! Who goes there?' would ring out when someone approached on a dark night. Back would come the answer. 'Dick.' Then the person on guard would say, 'Advance one and be circumcised!' This rather crude but comical combination of words may not have been exactly in Battalion Standing Orders, but it worked and I'm sure the Chinese would never have cracked the home-made code. It was also a fact that by and large we could recognized the voices of men in our platoon or company. Having said that, it was rumoured that a Black

Watch patrol had returned from one mission only to find that a Chinese soldier had tagged on the end of the group and, in the dark, had caused a few problems.

There was also the case within our Battalion where one patrol got lost and ended up coming back through our lines at the wrong place. Apparently, they were a bit slow answering the challenge and a grenade was thrown, but fortunately it was well wide of the mark, which goes to show that war is not an exact science, though politicians and other commentators often talk as if it were.

Eventually, in late February, the day arrived when we were told to pack our bags and move out. It was all done rather hurriedly and before we knew it we were piled into 3-ton trucks and were heading down dusty roads to a new destination, we knew not where. On the way we had a very narrow escape when our vehicle slewed on a mountain bend and the back ended up hanging over a drop. Everyone quickly edged to the front end, the driver put his foot down and, thankfully, disaster was averted. At the time everyone was so excited about going into reserve that this incident was treated as a big joke, although on reflection it was anything but. Such is war.

Chapter 15

Reserve Destination, Burying the Dead and Boxing

On arrival at the reserve destination, we were split into groups and allocated an area where we could dig our bunkers. As a temporary measure, whilst we dug in, we were housed in rather crude huts. It was a case of dumping your kitbag on the floor and picking 6ft of space to put your sleeping bag down – and that was it! Despite this, there was no doubt about it, this was real luxury and we were all looking forward to a full night's sleep without being woken at some unearthly hour to do a guard duty or man our communication systems. There was also the privilege of sleeping inside your sleeping bag instead of on top of it and the utter pleasure of taking your boots off.

We were told that in the first week we would be excused all duties and allowed to sleep whenever we wanted. This was five-star treatment at its best. The result of these concessions turned out to be quite remarkable. Some of the lads literally slept for days, only briefly crawling out of their sleeping bags to get some food, but what took nearly everyone by surprise was the reaction we all felt after about two or three days rest. Almost everyone who had been in the front line got the shakes, as it's called. Quite a number of the lads came to me and held their hands out. 'Look at that,' they exclaimed, and as they stretched out their arms and hands you could see them tremble. Everyone soon realized it was the reaction to months of sleeplessness and tension, but at first they thought it was some kind of medical condition.

Once we were settled in I decided to pick a good spot for my bunker and at the same time I struck a deal with a friend of mine called Moustache Pearson who was known throughout the Division – Corporal Pearson had grown the greatest piece of fungus any of us had ever seen. It had outstripped all other attempts to grow this handlebar type of facial adornment, so that you only had to say 'Corporal Moustache' and everyone would know exactly who you meant. We both agreed that we would help each other dig one bunker each, but we would live in the first one whilst we dug the second. This speeded things up and some of the two-handed jobs such as fetching logs were more easily dealt with. We also bonded our sandbags as well, so the finished results were very good.

Once we started digging we soon found that the area we were in had been some kind of battleground or killing field. At regular intervals corpses were found and it was at this time I learned that hair carries on growing after you are dead, or so it seemed. We dug up one Korean body which had hair right down to his shoulders and his state of preservation was so good it was hard to believe he really was dead, but the sickly sweet smell whilst undertaking this task is something that is never forgotten. In order to rationalize the situation from a hygiene point of view, orders were given for a large pit to be dug, into which all the corpses were put, limed over and then it was filled in.

The digging of the bunkers was a good keep-fit exercise which most of us enjoyed. The weather was now becoming much warmer and our previous experience erecting bunkers was put to good use. Not far away was a clump of pine trees so we were able to line our bunkers like log cabins. Picture frames were made from odd bits of wood and cartoons and sketches, or whatever, were soon hung around the walls. As the second bunker neared completion, Moustache Pearson made a very unwelcome discovery. From various tell-tale signs it was almost certain that deep down below the bunker there was a body. The thought of spending another week digging and building on a fresh spot – perhaps even to find the same thing – did not seem a very good option. What to do? After much deliberation we decided to plank the floor and let the matter rest.

In retrospect this might seem a harsh decision, but we were only in reserve for one month, so this seemed the most sensible expedient. Once the decision was made it was surprising how easily the situation was accepted. Sleeping on what was a grave is not something people normally do, but war often turns normal thinking on its head. One of the floor planks near the door was rather springy and it became a standard saying for anyone entering the bunker to exclaim, 'Sorry George!' This might seem slightly irreverent but in actual fact what it meant was that George had become one of us. Whoever was down there had paid the ultimate price, as indeed any one of us might have to do.

During the first period in reserve it was decided that a boxing match would be arranged between C Company and Support Company. As a Regimental Signaller, I was classed as a Support Company soldier. Since this consisted of the Assault Pioneers, Transport, Machine Gun and Mortar Platoons, we had plenty of lads to choose from, and with Captain Swift in charge we were soon sweating up and down hills, undergoing sessions of skipping, punchbag and sparring practice. I was duly enrolled in the heavyweight division which was remarkable because my weight was normally around 12 stone to 12 stone 6lb. Eating to keep warm in the winter had made everyone put on weight, but the pounds soon came off as we ran the miles and sweated. I enjoyed the training immensely and the sparring was good fun. All the team took turns in fighting each other so that there were some lively contests. I found that Corporal Oram's training had given me such a good grounding that I could hold my own with any of the team.

On one particular day I had just finished a few rounds when one of the sergeants watching stepped into the ring and said, 'Leave the gloves on, Nev, I'd like a couple of rounds.' Knowing that he had been pretty good in his day, I decided to test him with a few straight lefts and one or two jabs, to see what his reaction would be. He was obviously an all-action fighter because he came in ducking and weaving like a professional, so we were soon enjoying a good bout. Suddenly, as we went into a clinch, he whispered in my ear, 'Go easy will you, I'm knackered.' After this we waltzed and danced our way through the round, after which he took the gloves off and thanked me. Afterwards he said that he couldn't believe how out of condition he was. In his mid to late thirties, my sergeant sparring partner had found out a home truth we all have to learn eventually. What you could once do is not necessarily what you can do today. Now in my late seventies as I write this story, I find it hard to believe how unwilling my body is to act and move when I think of those far-off days. I still exercise each day and keep fit for my age, but what a joy it once was when I could run, skip, jump and move with such ease. Was it really me who used to do a day's work, go three evenings a week to night school and do an hour's training when I arrived home? Or play a game of football then dance the night away? Such is life!

The day of the actual boxing matches arrived and a very competitive affair it turned out to be. First C Company would win a fight, then Support Company would win one. Captain Swift had a terrific set to with one of C Company's best lads and was hard put to shave a points decision. Eventually my turn came, but I had no idea about my opponent's credentials. Although I was confident, this was my first competitive fight. My opponent was a big lad called Ford who seemed well muscled, but after about half a minute of boxing I realized he had not been as well taught as I had. I could tell by his footwork and the way he covered up that he would not be too difficult to outbox. Once we had exchanged a few blows I knew his punch was not as hard as mine, so I was pretty sure I could win the fight, as long as I didn't take any silly chances.

By the end of the first round I was sure I had a good lead on points. In the second round Ford came out as if he meant business, but he made one of the worst mistakes you can make in boxing – he actually jumped in with both feet off the ground and when I hit him with a hard straight left he went flat on his back. He got up rather shaken and I knew then I had the fight won. I had no intention of going for a knockout because, after all, we were here to fight the Chinese. Victory in this fight meant that I would be in the Battalion Boxing Team the next time we went in reserve, but that is another story.

One of our team was a man called Stevens and he really was good. I'm sure he could have turned pro. A two-handed fighter who could throw combination punches, he easily won his fight and was later chosen as team captain. I enjoyed sparring with him and found I could hold my own, but when he entered the ring for a contest he definitely moved up a notch or two.

Later, when I received a copy of the battalion magazine which was published in the UK, copies of which were sent up the line to us, I was given a good write-up regarding our inter-company boxing match. I was a bit surprised to read: 'LCpl Williams won his fight with an exhibition of neat footwork and clean punching.' Of course, what little skill I had was all down to my friend Corporal Oram, now killed in action. 'Always keep solid on your feet,' he would say, 'or you can't punch your weight. Never throw a punch unless you mean it,' was another bit of good advice. 'Punch from the shoulder and keep your wrist straight. Use a left hook when you can because your left hand is nearest your opponent, but keep your chin in to avoid counter punches.' 'Never cross your legs,' was another no-no, 'but if you see your opponent do so, go for him because he can't punch properly with legs crossed.' All good advice.

I believed, and still do, that boxing is a manly art and, when carried out under proper control, is a sport the basics of which all youngsters should be taught. As long as opponents are matched weight for weight and have similar abilities, and there is a referee who can step in where necessary, then it teaches the valuable lessons of managing to accept success and failure, the need to have a fit body and the courage to face an opponent in a confined area, where there is no chance to run away; and also to give and take a blow with a good spirit. More often than not, two boxers who have had a good bout will be the best of friends afterwards.

During the bout I was pleased to see my mate Jim Sibeon win his fight and later we were both in the Battalion Team. He was a tough little all-action fighter who always gave the audience their money's worth.

During our reserve period I got a very unusual job to do which really taxed my artistic abilities, but which turned out to be quite successful. At the same time it also provided a bit of fun which could never have happened in barracks.

On one bright sunny day the Adjutant sent the Sergeant Major to ask me if I could, by some means, make a fairly large crown, with battle honours under it, such that it would fit beneath the battalion flag. The idea was that there would be an area below the flag about 4ft square, with a square sloping wall filled with soil. Into this area the emblem of the crown taken from our cap badge would fit. The dates represented the sea battle when Welsh troops on board fought off an enemy for which the King gave them the honour of wearing a crown with his personal motto 'ich dien' on it. After a bit of head scratching I decided to make the crown and dates out of beer bottle tops. This might have seemed a tall order to collect a couple of hundred tops, but not so – the Sergeants' Mess tent was not far away and this proved to be an ideal hunting grounds. Within a couple of days I had reached my target so the next task was to borrow a hammer and tap them square. This done, I prepared an earth bed on the hillside the same size as the one under the flag, into which I neatly fashioned the crown and dates. I was surprised how effective it looked even before the tops were painted, but once complete it was hard to believe that the finished product was made of discarded bottle tops. To make reassembly under the flag easier, I numbered each piece, popped them in a bag and set off for HQ.

When I reported to the Adjutant he told me not to discuss or give any indication of what I was doing, but to direct any enquiries to him. For a moment I did not quite understand what he was up to, but then it dawned on me what a giant leg-pull this exercise could be. Normally anyone found sitting under the flag, as I would be doing, would be marched off and charged. In army slang, 'Their feet wouldn't touch the ground.' However, here I was sat under the flag like some simpleton, putting pretty stones in the soil. Because the pieces were numbered I was able to make up the design in stages so that it wasn't immediately recognizable. Sure enough, I had hardly started when a captain from the machine-gun section turned up and told me to stop what I was doing whilst he bowled into the Adjutant's hut across the square. Within a couple of minutes both came out laughing and I got the thumbs up.

During the morning I almost lost count of the number of officers and NCOs who were beguiled by this joke and I had almost finished the layout before it became apparent what I was doing. Of course these officers almost invariably brought some other gullible person to see what I was doing. I was soon able to perfect my act of pretence that I was only half with it, so a good morning's fun was had by all. Outside of active service conditions this sort of situation would never have been tolerated. The completed design was quite pleasing and remained in position whilst we were in reserve.

On a more serious note, a situation arose about this time which in retrospect showed quite clearly how ordinary National Servicemen could become hardened fighting men, who could be tempted to do things they would never have dreamed possible in civvy street. On a hillside near where we were dug in, one of the lads discovered the body of a Chinese or North Korean soldier who had been incinerated by napalm or a flame-thrower. He had obviously been running away when he had been hit and his charred remains lay spreadeagled, face down, with arms and legs outstretched in a star shape – a very macabre sight and not something you see every day. Very sad – very eerie. As we walked up to the body, one of the lads called Mc something, started kicking the remains. The rest of us were not impressed and for once I pulled rank and told him to pack it in. On reflection, I think he realized what he was doing was out of order, but an incident like this does show how war can change people. Never in his wildest dreams could our friend ever have imagined himself kicking a corpse about. What was left of the body was eventually put in one of the lime pits. Would anyone even know who he was? No doubt someone, somewhere, was hoping for his return.

Things were never dull whilst we were in reserve and on one particular occasion we were given the task of cutting down a very large tree. It was probably some 3ft in diameter and when stripped of its branches was still a large and heavy piece of timber. I have forgotten why but the officer who requested it wanted about 20ft of the main bowl of the tree. Several of us were pretty good with an axe by this time, so felling a tree and trimming it was no big deal, but moving this monster was an entirely different matter. We tried log rollers, pushing, pulling, rolling and various other methods involving brute force and ignorance. Eventually, my good friend Kim took a hand, signalling for us to step aside whilst he gathered about a dozen of his porter friends. Initially they spent a little time gathering some ropes made of platted rice straw, then the men positioned themselves in pairs either side of the giant log. Kim gave us a knowing grin then gave the order to start. With the ropes passed under the log and each porter holding the ends via his shoulders, all the men began to chant and sway. As the chant got louder the men began to sway more and more until suddenly as one man they let out a sound that probably meant heave, and each of them in perfect formation moved forward. Low and behold this enormous log began to move and the process was repeated over and over again until it lay in position at the bottom of the hill. The combination of rhythm and movement was quite awesome and put our feeble efforts to shame. As an engineer I was much impressed and this incident clearly showed what can be done by a few people working in harmony and unison.

Many years later when I was a training officer in charge of large workshops, one of my apprentices won the Great Britain pattern-making competition, which made him eligible for the world championships in Spain. He did not win, as chance would have it, but received a commendation. It was a Korean, however, who actually won the event. When I asked our representative what made the Korean better than all the other competitors, he said that the pattern they were asked to make was not only complicated, but required the removal of a lot of wood to get at the final shape. The Korean surprised everyone by taking his shoes off and, by holding the wood with his feet, he used an old-fashioned adze to hack out the main shape. Using this ancient method, the Korean had his work piece near to size before the other competitors had barely commenced, thus leaving himself plenty of time for finishing the project.

From what I saw in Korea I had no doubt that the people had an innate skill to make things, their patient and careful approach to problems being a great asset. Now in the twenty-first century, Koreans are recognized as hard-working, master craftsmen, who are fast overtaking many Western countries in their ability to manufacture quality goods.

Shortly after the log incident, Lieutenant Brindlecombe got one or two of us together to see if we could muster a couple of scratch rugby teams. He had been my officer during the winter and I knew he was keen on rugby and would not object to a rough house. The idea was that we would pick two teams and assemble them one on each of two small hills with a valley in between. A small rag ball was to be placed in the valley area and, at a command from Lieutenant Brindlecombe, the teams would converge on the ball, each with the aim of carrying it back to the top of their hill. What a brilliant, crazy idea. In no time at all we were all mixed up in a milieu, struggling to find the ball and keep it. Bushes and shrubs made it virtually impossible to know who had the ball and if anyone did appear to have it they were nearly torn apart. At one point in the game, Lieutenant Bridlecombe was daft enough, or brave enough depending on how you viewed the game, to hold on to the ball and was dragged all over the place. Eventually someone yelled, 'We've won!' but I think they were on the wrong hill. The hilarious game was only played once because I think the Lieutenant realized it had the potential to do some real damage to the players. As it was, it was just a case of scratched elbows and knees plus a few swollen whatevers. Everyone enjoyed the exercise immensely and went away laughing and joking about their particular experiences in this 'anything goes' match.

Although we were in reserve there was the need for regular guard duties on the dusty road which led in and out of our positions. I didn't mind doing the odd duty, but at one period I was called on to do three in one week. I didn't subscribe to this so I went to see our Regimental Sergeant Major. He didn't particularly know me because he had been at HQ and he thought I had been in reserve all the while, but when I explained I had been in the most forward position he apologized and promptly took me off the roster. This was another example of the difference between soldiering in active and peacetime conditions.

Towards the end of our stay in reserve, Lieutenant Brindlecombe formed a battalion choir and, as previously described, we ended up giving a concert to the Norfolks, the Korean song 'Ardy Dong' being our hilarious finale.

The boxing, the training for it, the bunker building and various other asides were all a welcome break from our spell in the line but, like all good things, they had to come to an end. In what seemed no time at all we were soon packing our bags and heading back up the line to a famous battleground, Hill 355, nicknamed 'Little Gibraltar' because of its size and shape. The hill and surrounding area had been the scene of some very fierce fighting.

Before finally leaving our reserve site a game of basketball had been arranged with the Royal Artillery. I had played a reasonable amount of basketball during physical training sessions for football prior to joining up, and got into the team as a defender. I could defend and dribble, but whilst I could score baskets, shooting was not my strong point. When army sides meet at sport there is always a certain amount of 'needling', or what might be called pride in the regiment. This particular match was held on a bulldozed site, neither side being sure what the outcome would be. Fortunately for us our Sergeant PTI was an extremely good goal shooter, so we developed a simple master plan which worked like a charm. Defend with everyone back, but on breaking out, dribble, pass, or do what you want, but get the ball to our PTI for shooting. By the time the other team realized how good our Sergeant was we were well ahead. We went on to win the match but I got the feeling that the gunners were a bit shell shocked because being farther back than our lads they had been able to put in a lot more practice. There was talk of an athletics match, but the Battalion's front-line call to duty didn't allow it.

Chapter 16

Hill 355 and a True 'Thunderbox'

Just before leaving for Hill 355, I was told I would be attached to the Mortar Platoon, along with two south Wales National Servicemen, called Terry Hache and Di Davies. (Later we had another Di Davies join us, but he wasn't of the calibre of our initial Di.) Terry and I were to become great friends and his knowledge of bricklaying together with mine of engineering enabled us to build eventually one of the best, if not the best, command bunkers in the Battalion.

The Mortar Platoon was situated slightly below and to the right of Hill 355. A mountain rather than a hill, 355 stood out on the skyline, very much like Gibraltar. It was probably 1,500ft high, the top section being almost solid rock. I couldn't have known when we arrived, but I was to experience many desperate, hard and dangerous days laying and repairing telephone lines which ran up the back of this hill. It was one of the favourite places the Chinese loved to mortar and shell, a fact which nearly cost me my life.

Jim Sibeon and Lamacraft had both been allocated to companies, Jim being situated literally on top of 355. Every now and then we met up and swapped stories and information. We had all been saddened by the death of Arthur Rowe, a young National Serviceman who had joined up at the same time as us and had been with us right through our training in the UK. Jim Sibeon and Lamacraft had also both come near to disaster, shortly after they moved onto 355, but in a very unusual way.

Apparently, several of the lads were in one of the bunkers chatting when one of them carelessly pulled a pin on one of the grenades they had been priming. Fortunately, there was an adjoining bunker, they all scattered 'sharpish', as they say, and it went off without injuring anyone. Maybe it was a case of familiarity breeds contempt. Before we were to complete our stay in Korea the Battalion was to lose thirty-two men killed and over one hundred wounded, plus many men injured by everyday accidents and conditions. One death which struck me particularly forcibly was that of a Private Harris.

1ST BATTALION WELCH REGIMENT POSITIONS IN THE AREA OF HILL 355 (LITTLE GIBRALTAR) 18TH APRIL 1952 TO 8TH AUGUST 1952

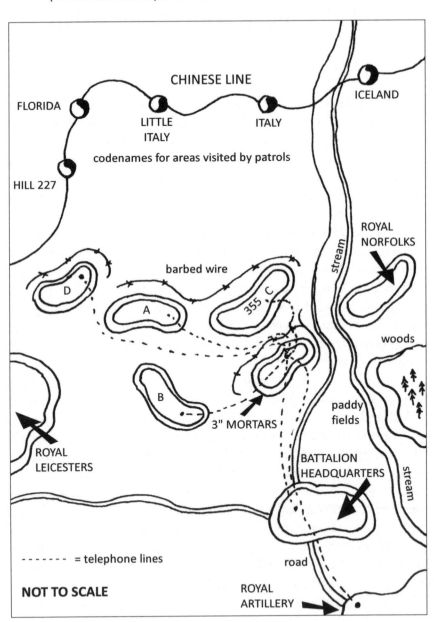

During the winter he had been loaned to us for about a month to help man our radios. He was a Devon lad who had a rich Devon accent and was well known for his moustache and broad grin. Always cheerful and full of life, I found it very difficult to believe a stray shell had taken him away. Harassing fire, as they called it, was an ever-present danger and like us the Chinese would often drop a few shells or mortars at dinnertimes or other periods when things seemed quiet and when the lads might be off their guard.

I have often wondered since what families must have thought and felt. Called up for National Service and sent to the other side of the world, young men would lose their lives in a forgotten war. It must have broken many mothers' hearts.

Never rear your son to be a soldier

Never rear your son to be a soldier
Never rear your son to fire a gun
Nor to put a musket to his shoulder
To go and fight some other mother's son.
Let all the kings of all the countries go and fight
Their wars and settle all their dirty matters too.
For there would be no wars today
If every mother would say,
'I'll never rear my son to be a soldier'.

Why should we fight when we know it isn't right?
Brothers we should be.
Why raise your gun to kill some other mother's son
And cause her endless agony
The poppies at the Flanders are sending a message far over the seas
saying,
Mothers, keep your son away from shells and guns
Then we'll live in peace eternally.

Let the man that made the gun fire the gun,
Let the man that made the shell fire the shell,
Let the man that made the poisonous gas
Take a whiff or two.
Then dress them up in khaki and see what they can do.

> For it's the profiteer who always wins the day,
> And we're the bloody mugs who have to pay
> And there would be no wars today
> If every mother would say,
> 'I'll never rear my son to be a soldier'.

This poem was common knowledge, especially amongst regulars, and must have come from the First World War. Although it would be classed as seditious, it was well known and when recited, it would receive nods of approval. 'Aye, that's right enough,' someone would say but it did not affect anyone's resolve or morale. If only life was as simple as the poem states. Or is it?

There are many sayings which are handed down in the Army. Often a bit crude but usually to the point and which have their origins in shared hardship. In the Welch Regiment a favourite saying was, 'Stick it the Welch'. Sometimes a couple of the lads would pass each other on the road after a hard night on patrol or in pouring rain, and one of them would say, 'Stick it the Welch'. Back would come a suitable reply like, 'Up yours', and both men would feel that much better.

When we took up our new position near Hill 355 we were greeted by the Americans who were moving out. They had occupied these positions for some time and were glad to be on the move. Our handover lasted a few days so we were able to exchange information and have a few laughs. They were an easy-going, friendly bunch, but to us they seemed a bit slap-happy. The bunkers they were leaving were not as well made as ours and they seemed to have a surplus of food which they did not bury and burn like us, so there was a very active rat population when we arrived. We knew this unhealthy situation would have to be addressed once they left, as indeed it was.

In the handover period we were slightly intrigued by one of their signallers, who was a black man. In those days coloured people in the Army were unheard of in Britain, but the Americans had quite a number of these enlisted men. Chalky White, as they called him, was a very likeable character and we enjoyed his company immensely. I think he enjoyed our easy acceptance, but it was noticeable that the white Americans treated him with a little less respect than they did for the other white Americans. It was not easy to put your finger on but there was definitely an 'us and them' situation.

The most striking feature of our new home was its 'scorched-earth' appearance. It was obvious that the position had been subjected to heavy shelling and mortar fire, because everywhere you looked there were shattered trees and damaged shrubs so that the landscape resembled that of the front during the First World War. Before we were to leave these positions we were to get more than a taste of this type of bombardment.

As soon as the Yanks moved out we set to work tidying up the site to make it safe and more habitable. Terry Hache and I enlarged our bunker and built some picket beds with wooden strips as a base. We intended to pad these out, but found we got used to sleeping on them, and that's how we managed for the next few months. Deep swill pits were dug and rat poison was spread around, but there was one incident with rats which was quite remarkable. One of the lads found a rat's nest in one bunker, so a number of his mates gathered round with fixed bayonets to try and skewer the mother rat as she collected her young, one by one. They chased her as she carried each one away quite some distance, returning again and again to collect another baby, bravely dodging the bayonets as she ran the gauntlet. In this way the little mother eventually rescued all her brood. Although it may have seemed a bit crude to try and bayonet these rodents, there was no doubt they were dangerous. Shortly after moving into our new positions there was an incident which illustrated quite clearly the danger which could come from rat infestation, and I have mentioned this problem before.

One bright morning Sergeant Bingham, the Mortar Sergeant, came over to me looking very concerned. He was carrying a tin box inside of which was his army beret. Offering it to me he asked, 'Can you see anything on the sweat band?' Funny question! But yes, I could. There were microscopic white dots which seemed to move. Then he told me why he was concerned. He had woken up that morning to find a rat nibbling his leather sweat band in his beret. The rat quickly scampered away, but left behind these unwanted guests. The only thing to do was to seal the hat in the tin box and sent it to the ADS (Advance Dressing Station) to be checked out. A day or so later the report came back. Yes, they were active microbes and yes, they were the type which could blind you. A narrow escape. Interestingly, when the lads were trying to bayonet the mother rat, they could, if they had wished to, shot it but I think a measure of natural justice took over because of the rat's bravery and this allowed the little pest to survive.

It was round about the time Sergeant Bingham had his nasty rat experience, Terry Hache, with whom I shared a bunker, also had a rat experience that would make your hair curl. On the night in question, I returned about midnight to our bunker and was just entering when I heard a sudden scuffling sound. As I quickly put the wire into our worn-out Heath-Robinson battery lighting arrangement (this involved connecting used batteries in series then linking them to torch bulbs), I was just in time to see a rat scurry away and witness Terry leaping off his machine-gun belt bed. Muttering unmentionable oaths he grabbed his rifle yelling, 'I'll kill it – I'll kill it!' It was some minutes before he calmed down enough to explain that he had woken up just as I came in, only to find a rat nibbling a speck of jam or food at the corner of his mouth, which must have been there when he went to bed. In the darkness the rat must have smelt the tiny morsel and was about to enjoy it when I came in and disturbed it. If Terry could have caught the rat at that time it would have suffered the death of a thousand knives. The thought of this incident still makes me cringe a bit, especially when you consider this experience was bought for the princely sum of one pound ten shillings (£1.50) per week. I think that's what they mean by 'insult to injury'.

With the Americans gone, we not only tidied up the site and improved our bunkers and dug swill pits, but we also built a new command bunker, which was definitely a state-of-the-art affair. We completely lined the roof and sides of the bunker with logs from the fir trees across the valley but, more importantly, the sandbag walls were laid using a Dutch bond, double thickness, with the middle of the walls filled with earth. Terry Hache being a bricklayer knew all about building walls so it was quite natural for him to think in terms of the various bonds. He gave me some quick lessons and in no time at all our masterpiece was taking shape. Later on a number of officers from the various companies dropped in and were much impressed with our efforts. The principles we had used were later adopted on various sites. Besides a strong roof on our bunkers we also made sure we had plenty of rocks on top so that if shells or mortars landed they would explode before they penetrated. This was particularly important with regard to the mortar bomb bays which could have over a 100 bombs in them ready for instant use.

Reroofing the bomb bays was a number one priority which more than paid off within two weeks of our arrival. Besides our work on bunkers, wiring was always high on the priority list and on one clear morning three of us were laying some barbed wire when our attention was drawn to the hills on our right. The Norfolks were occupying these when at about 1000 hrs the Chinese decided that they should become the target for the day. Shells and mortar bombs literally peppered the tops of the hills where they were dug in, but for us it was like watching a film. However, you didn't have to be a mathematician to work out that if the bombardment was lifted a few degrees and moved a few degrees to the right, then we would be due for the same treatment. Suddenly we felt the buzz in our ears that meant not only were we being shelled, but that the shells were right on target – us.

As one man, the three of us dived into one of the many slit trenches which dotted our hillside. I was in second and one of the Liverpool lads was third, but the lad who landed first had the very doubtful privilege of having the two of us land on top of him. I forget their names now, but I do remember the first lad giving us a good cursing. As the other lad said, 'What did you expect us to do – wave to them?' When we finally emerged, we realized what a close squeak we had just had. The shell had actually landed on one of the bomb bays, but the rocks had absorbed the explosion before it penetrated. Had we left the bomb bays in the state the Americans had handed them over, it was possible half the platoon could have been killed or injured.

After this close shave we made our way back to our bunkers whilst the Chinese practised zeroing up on our new positions. After a couple of hours of this unwelcomed barrage, our lads gave the Chinese a taste of their own medicine. These exchanges were to become a regular feature of our stay in this area. With experience we became quite expert at judging where shells and mortars were likely to land. If they screamed overhead at a certain tone we knew they would land in the paddy fields behind us, where they would sink in and blow a 6ft hole. Shells hitting the top of our hill were the most dangerous and there were many close calls. If the scream had a certain 'zip' about it, we knew it was quite near. If we were unlucky enough to get a thump on our eardrums it was likely to be in our back pocket. Shells which overshot our positions were relatively safe because the blast would send most of the shrapnel forward, but if they landed ahead of us then debris would fly all around us. Mortar bombs, of course, were a different matter. They made a different sound to the shells and the fallout from them would scatter in all directions. Day or night the Chinese would send over harassing fire hoping to catch us napping, at mealtimes particularly, but we got used to this and we would eat our dinner or lunch in our bunkers.

Our observation bunker on Hill 355 was used to direct our mortar fire on the enemy and, gradually by adjustment, our lads could pinpoint any enemy movement. The telephone lines to these particular bunkers had to be maintained at all times which did, on occasions, lead to some very hairy moments for Terry Hache and myself. Only a couple of days after taking up position, Hill 355 received a fair old barrage from the Chinese which caused dozens of telephone lines to be blown apart. What a mess! Tracing our broken ends was, to say the least, difficult but at least it gave me a chance to meet some of my old mates.

Hill 355 had been the site of some serious fighting during the winter and the first thing that struck us when we arrived on top was the Chinese dead hanging on the wire in front of the hill. During the winter the cold had refrigerated these corpses so that burying them was not a priority, and maybe the Yanks thought they might act as a warning to those that followed. Whatever the reasons for leaving them, the warmer weather which we were now appreciating was causing them to smell – the only answer was therefore to collect them and bury them properly, but what a job! The lads involved were glad to see it done and finished with – and all for £1.50 a week. My old mate Jim Sibeon wasn't exactly pleased to be involved, even though in civvy street he was a joiner who used to do part-time work for his undertaker uncle. Jim had an impish sense of humour and for some reason (probably because he was a joiner) he used to carry a measuring tape in his pocket. If he saw one of the lads having a nap he would sometimes get his tape out and start measuring him up. Although it was only a joke, they would sometimes get up and tell him to knock it off, or words to that effect.

When I joined the Mortar Platoon as a signaller I knew very little about this particular ordnance. I had fired a 2-inch mortar, but these larger 3-inch mortars were a different kettle of fish. They had a range of some 3,000yds, and the mortar crews were highly trained and very efficient. If the call 'stand-to' was given, the mortar crews would drop whatever they were doing and race to their allotted mortar pits, each member of a crew taking up his position within seconds. Their reaction time was similar to that of a fireman going to a fire. Once the command 'bombs away' was given, there would be a deafening explosion, followed by further cries of 'bombs in' and 'bombs away'. When firing occurred at night the mortars would give a 40ft flash as the bomb detonated and flew out of the barrel. Very impressive. Shortly after settling in we had one incident during a hasty 'stand-to' which could have come out of a Charlie Chaplin film.

The Chinese had started shelling Hill 355, so the message had been passed down for our lads to return fire. As the men raced to their mortar bays two shells landed near one of our field toilets. This particular latrine had sacking tied to poles to give a bit of privacy, however, from the scuffling inside it was obvious one of the lads was in the process of using it. At this very moment one of the mortar crew got their first bomb away, which turned out to be a creeper. These were bombs with either a faulty or wet charge in them, which caused them to go off like a damp squib. Usually they only landed 40 or 50yds away, although in theory they would not explode because there was a mechanism in the bomb which only activated it after it reached a certain height. In this case, however, the lad using the toilet had heard the creeper which landed near him, at the same time as a Chinese shell landed. The shock must have been considerable because he emerged dragging his trousers up and with a cut on his chin from a fragment of the shell; at the same time he was staggering and running to get into his mortar pit. Did he get a rousing cheer! Later, when the action was over, he told me that he thought the creeper bomb had exploded, not realizing it was a Chinese shell. The cut on his chin was not too serious but a very unpleasant reminder of a close shave. What an experience! Even Sergeant Bingham had a job to stop laughing as he urged his late arrival to get into his mortar pit.

Within a few weeks, Terry Hache and I not only improved our sleeping accommodation, but had also built a very large command bunker fitted out in a similar manner. Furniture was fashioned from old boxes and our telephone exchange was well set up with all our dozen or so lines clearly tagged and identified. I did some cheeky cartoons for the walls and, much to the delight of the lads, we rigged up a speaker from which we could play music for an hour or so each day, run off 12 volt batteries. These were collected every day for recharging, but we would use the odd few volts left in them for our entertainment. Our 62 sets had a very good range so we could usually find something for the men to listen to. Even the divisional padre, who used to come round about once per month, was much impressed by our set-up and needed little persuading to stop and have a cup of tea.

Chapter 17

The Bombardment and a May Day Surprise

During late April a curious state of affairs occurred, which gave us all cause for concern. Quite inexplicably the Chinese stopped bombarding us and hardly any shots were fired. This went on for about eight days and, quite naturally, we thought they were preparing for an all-out offensive. This condition gave us that eerie sort of feeling that you get when you expect bad news from a doctor, or someone fails to answer a letter, which is critical to your well-being.

What we had not reckoned with, or remembered to take into account, was the importance of May Day, which is the communist red letter day. The Chinese were about to give us a salutary reminder.

At 1200 hrs on 1 May, the Chinese opened up with everything that could reach us and for the next four or five hours the air was full of screaming metal as shells and mortar bombs rained down on us. It was estimated that well over a 1,000 shells fell on the Battalion in that short period. Crouching in our bunkers, all we could do was sit and wait for the bombardment to stop. As shells or mortars landed close by, the bunker roofs would shake and sprinkle soil down on us. We joked and waited, willing the barrage to stop, but apprehensive that when it did there would be heavy casualties. Eventually our own 25-pounders, which were a few miles behind the lines, began pounding away and I think that this probably influenced the situation, but whatever the reason, around about teatime the shelling ceased. Amazingly, we found out that the Battalion had only suffered one dead and I don't know how many injured. One dead was one too many, yet after such a heavy attack it was hard to believe the situation wasn't worse. Without doubt, the quality of our bunkers must have played an important part in saving many lives.

For the next few days we were kept very busy mending broken telephone lines, some of which were blown yards apart, as well as being hopelessly entangled. The bright side of this was that it gave me a chance to meet some of my old mates in the different companies. All had hair-raising tales to tell, but at lease we were alive and kicking.

In mid-May our battle-scarred landscape was to pass through one of nature's miraculous transformations. We had heard the word monsoon used from time to time, but we were ill-prepared for the real thing. When it rained in the UK it generally just rained and then stopped, but with the monsoon period it was an entirely different kettle of fish.

It started as a warm, fine drizzle, which gradually increased in intensity. Because the rain was not cold it didn't seem too bad at first and we decided it would stop the next day. But the next day came and went and the day after, and the next day too, so by day four or five, everywhere became a mud bath and the water ran down the hillside in streams, which soon filled up the monsoon gutters dug at the sides of the bulldozed roads. Bunkers became waterlogged so many of the lads were forced to move out and share with anyone whose bunkers were still holding out. Our command bunker was coping, but by the second week our sleeping bunker began to seep water through the walls, even though the roof held.

Out of some forty-eight men on our site, we all eventually ended up in about twelve bunkers. Everyone trudged around in shorts and boots – we didn't bother with shirts – whilst the rain seemed to fall with a steady constancy which began to make you wonder if it would ever stop. Now and again you would hear the squealing of tyres as the driver tried to extract his vehicle from the mud. The cook managed to keep the cookhouse working so our meals weren't too bad, if a bit soggy at times. The spirit of survival is always something to be marvelled at, and so it was at this time. Perhaps one consolation was our enemy was also suffering the same conditions.

As in many walks of life when adversity strikes, people often make light of the situation by joking. So it was with us. The phone would ring and a voice would say, 'Hello, this is the *Empire Fowey*, Captain speaking!' (the *Fowey* being the boat that had brought us to Korea). Other remarks would be related to swimming. 'I'll be with you shortly, I'm just swimming down the main road, but I've stopped to do a bit of sunbathing.' One classic was the Sergeant's dismissal after having a meeting to check how things were going. 'Right lads. Turn to your right and fall out, but keep walking when your hat floats. Goodbye!'

After about two weeks of this incessant rain the streams and gutters were raging torrents and all our equipment and kit were soaked but, fortunately, the downpours stopped before we were completely overwhelmed and the sun broke through to dry us all out. We had now experienced four of Korea's six climate extremes: the 'two' cold, 'two' wet and now we were to experience the 'two' hot.

As the sun began to dry up the run-off and mud, so the air became humid. It was what might be called greenhouse weather. It is strange to look back and remember those days because never before or since have I experienced such vapour-laden air. It was so humid at times that if you called to a friend 20yds away your voice would seem to fall to the ground and quite often they would not hear you. With the advent of these conditions came the rebirth of nature in all its abundance. Trees, flowers, bushes, grasses and all the birds and insects which had been hibernating, all suddenly sprang to life. At night you could hear a constant rustle as the undergrowth moved and grew. Out of curiosity we measured some plants and found that they would grow as much as an inch in the night. Golden orioles nested nearby and were often seen flitting around the site, their yellow and black plumage adding colour to a fast-changing scene, for what had been a barren hillside was now turning into an almost tropical garden.

Dragonflies in their blues and greens appeared everywhere, while at night the very large bullfrogs in the paddy fields croaked their unending chorus. Although we got used to this endless noise, on occasions it would cease as if a conductor had raised his baton to indicate a pause. I often wondered if a snake had made its presence felt, because there were plenty about. Whatever the reason it always seemed a bit eerie when it happened. Ants and various beetles appeared at this time, including that very strange creature, the firefly. When they emerged at night it often seemed as if an enemy was about, walking with swinging lanterns. Hence the mistake made by a new officer who had his platoon 'stood to' because he thought it was indeed the enemy. This platoon was known thereafter as 'the firefly platoon'. Good for a laugh, except for those involved.

It was at this time that the dreaded mosquitoes arrived so that some of the lads had very swollen faces, hands and legs. Being rather hairy, I was not too bothered by these pests and I took the trouble to put plenty of anti-midge liquid on my hat and clothes. I also used to smear a bit of paraffin around my hat and at night, before I went to bed, I would pull my mosquito net down then sit with a lighted candle. Any mosquitoes caught inside the net would zip into the candle flame and get fried, so that if you sat for five minutes or so until the sizzling stopped, you could be pretty sure none were inside your mosquito netting. Most of the lads used this simple elimination technique, but for anyone who didn't, a swollen eye or similar was likely to be the outcome. The mosquitoes would obviously go for very tender, soft, fleshy parts so eyelids and cheeks were favourite morsels.

Around this time my mate Jim Sibeon got nicknamed 'Boto' because of his fascination with creatures great and small. I remember meeting him once when I was mending a line to C Company and he called me across to watch a beetle which was surrounded by a semi-circle of ants. Jim had put the beetle against a piece of wood in the ground so that when the ants from a nearby nest surrounded it, it couldn't escape except by passing through the swarm. A bit crude maybe, but fascinating. Jim said he had seen the same thing happen without his intervention. Suddenly, as if on a command, the ants all rushed in, each ant working to a purpose and in no time at all the beetle was subdued by their bites, had his legs severed and was being carried away in pieces. Shortly after this, I witnessed two dragonflies locked end to end possibly fighting or, more likely, mating and unaware of some approaching ants. The end result was very similar to that of the beetle – they were overcome, chopped up and carried away. What is it the Bible says? 'Consider the ways of the ant and be wise.' They certainly work as a team, each knowing place and purpose.

I have been a lover of the countryside, even as a youngster and teenager, and was lucky enough to be born near miles of open fields. Living on the outskirts of Chester I found it the most natural thing to roam the countryside with my friends. Sometimes I would get up at five or six in the morning and go mushrooming, or at other times I would collect wild fruit such as blackberries. In my summer holidays I relished the chance to go fruit picking, pea harvesting or potato lifting for the local market gardeners. It was hard work but it earned me a few shillings. In 1945 I'd saved enough to go to Manchester for the Victory Test Matches, where I saw great England players like Wally Hammond and Len Hutton, and Keith Miller of Australia.

I can still name nearly every British bird and, to my shame as a young teenager, I had a shared collection of some seventy birds' eggs. Of course we did understand the country better than many people now who only drive through it, so that when we took an egg for our collection we always took the last of the clutch. That way the bird would not desert the nest. Once we had one egg for our collection we would not take further eggs, but we did enjoy looking in the nests and watching the chicks grow. It is one of the marvels of nature to see how beautifully made are some of the nests of small birds. The circular, well-hidden nest of the wren, or the moss and feathered home of the chaffinch, are beautifully constructed. I wonder how many people know why the bullfinch is so named. What brave little birds they are. If we found one of their nests with a bird sitting on it we would slowly move a finger towards it. Most birds would fly away but not the bullfinch, which would sit tight and peck you. Of course in nature only a small percentage of young birds survive to become adults. Rats are particularly partial to eggs and I have looked in many a nest only to see broken shells. Other young birds are often picked off by predators and in some cases fish, like pike, will take young moorhens or anything which floats.

With the winter behind us, the rains departed and everything in full bloom, there were times when it would have been easy to forget there was a war on. That is, except for the nasty Chinese habit of dropping shells and mortar bombs on us at regular intervals. Each day we would go down to the paddy fields behind us and have a bath in a chopped-down oil drum, or sometimes we would take a shower under a picket and tin bucket arrangement. We even dammed up the nearby stream to make a swimming pool, which was very acceptable to everyone. Of course, you had to be wary of harassing fire, but much of it was fairly predictable and a lot of it was on the basis of one for you and one for me. There was, however, one occasion when our faithful Korean porter Kim had an incredibly close shave. On the particular day in question he was unwise enough to go for a bath at dinner time, a time when the CCPR (Chinese Communist People's Republic) tended to be very active.

Several of us sitting in the entrance to our bunkers had seen Kim disappear down the hill into the paddy fields, so that when the harassing fire flew overhead we knew he was in danger. One of the lads had no sooner said, 'Do you think Kim's all right?' than Kim burst upon the scene, running as if he was out to break a sprint record. As he ran he shouted, 'Number ten, number ten!' Later, when we went to see what had happened, we were amazed to find that a shell had landed right alongside the makeshift bath and had blown a 6ft hole in the paddy field. Fortunately for Kim the shell had sunk deep into the soft paddy field before exploding, so he had escaped unharmed, except that is for a bad attack of shock. He never went for a bath at dinner time after that episode.

Kim, along with the other porters, was well respected by all the lads. Hardworking, helpful, well mannered and very knowledgeable in the art of survival, he was a great asset. Along with his mates he did most of the laundry in the local stream and for larger items such as blankets, pummelled them with rocks. Even in cold water the Koreans could get our washing done to a high standard, reshaping and eliminating the creases before the clothes were dry. Kim soon recovered his normal self after the shell incident and was even able to laugh about it. Unlike us, the porters had been in the Korean War from its early stages so that their experience was invaluable. They would have to carry on after we had left and the pay they received was scant reward for enduring such a hard and dangerous life.

Whilst I enjoyed the wildlife in Korea I did not particularly like the snakes we sometimes saw. We were warned that most were harmless, other than the yellow and brown adder which was dangerous. The porters were well aware of which was which and I remember seeing them capture and play with some. There was one species which was about 6ft long, marked with alternate black and white ring markings, which appeared to me to be anything but harmless, but the porters would pick it up and usually pass it round between them before killing it. Kim said that even if you cut its head off it would wriggle and writhe until sundown, which on observation did seem to be the case. The yellow adder, most fortunately, was rare, but I did have one very unpleasant encounter with one. I was at the time tracing a broken telephone line which had become well covered with vegetation. Pulling the line to see where it lay I suddenly found myself about 3ft from a sleeping adder. He was at the base of a small tree and my presence must have woken him. I don't know who was the most scared, him or me. As I jumped back a couple of feet he uncoiled and sped off into the undergrowth, leaving me rather shocked. After that incident I was always a bit more careful going about my tasks.

There was also the case of one of our corporals meeting a snake rather unexpectedly when doing some wiring in the paddy fields.

Engrossed in his work he had turned round only to see a snake in the raised position about to strike. Startled he had rushed to the bank to grab his Sten gun only to find that the snake had slithered away. Fear turned to anger as he rushed back to the spot where he had last seen the reptile. Within seconds he had fired off a whole magazine all round him. Everyone else fell about laughing, but if he could have found that snake he would have killed it fifty times over.

We had been briefed that snakes usually strike at the ankles which was why we wore putties, but I had my doubts about that statement. A little while later our Corporal, who was terrified by a snake, formed one or two hunting parties to try to eliminate any in our immediate vicinity. I didn't particularly subscribe to this idea but I could understand his dislike of them.

There was also the scenario of some of our lads coming upon a fairly large snake when they were bathing in the pool. Apparently it was too close for comfort, but once again someone came up with a piece of doubtful information. It was said that if a snake was in water or drinking, its venom was not very active. I wouldn't have liked to have put that theory to the test.

Whilst on the subject of snakes, it is worth recounting Terry Hache's encounter. Unwanted and unexpected it certainly gave Terry a shock. It happened when he and I were out mending a broken line which passed through a small wood. As we traced the line we came to an area where it more or less followed a path through the wood. Terry and I often had serious discussions relating to life outside the Army and on this occasion I remember we were talking about money. We both agreed that when we got out it wouldn't be that important to us, only a means to an end. Friends and work would come first. Engrossed in our philosophical conversation we were suddenly startled by a flash of colour as a snake shot across Terry's foot. Whether it had struck and missed, or was just as alarmed as we were, we would never know, but for sure Terry was not amused. As often happens, shock quickly turns to anger when realization kicks in. So it was with Terry, and his rifle was off his shoulder in record time, but by then our slithering friend was nowhere to be seen. As the day progressed we could be forgiven for thinking this incident was an omen. The line we were tracking led parallel to the bottom of Hill 355, after which it rose vertically up the back of the hill to the command bunker telephone exchange. It was a fair old slog doing this and as we neared the bottom of the hill we were beginning to come under enemy mortar fire. Time and again we had to dive down as bombs landed and shrapnel rained down. At this time we knew that a detachment of lads from our mortar team were somewhere around giving the enemy a hard time, but we didn't know exactly where. Then, quite suddenly, we came across them in a small clearing. Their equipment was almost red hot as they had fired some 300 rounds. By moving their position it was hoped that the enemy would not know where the bombs originated. It was obvious, however, that by the time we reached the lads the Chinese were getting closer and closer and had not been fooled by their tactics. There was no time to waste and we had a quick word with our mates before once again resuming our task of finding the break in our telephone line. Halfway up the back of Hill 355 we found the break, but not before I had come close to being wounded. The shells and mortars from the Chinese were dropping with monotonous regularity by this time, and Terry and I were getting more than a bit concerned as we frequently dived down for cover. Suddenly, as a shell dropped some 30yds in front of us, I heard the unmistakable whizz of a piece of shrapnel as it sunk into the ground 3 or 4 inches from my head, which was pressed hard into the ground. If it had been slightly bigger it would have done some real damage, but a miss is as good as a mile, so it was up and away. Although the climb up the back of the hill was 1,000ft or more, the shelling gave wings to our feet and, once we had mended the break, we decided to just head for the top of the hill and forget any other breaks because when we rang back on the broken ends we found we could get back to our own site, but not to B Company command bunker. This meant there would be further breaks ahead and the odds were that the ends would be widely scattered, but by now it was far too unhealthy to hang around in the open. When we finally neared the summit it was, as we suspected, only worse. Upwards of a dozen lines had been laid side by side in the main communicating trench and these had received direct hits which had blown the ends in all directions. These would eventually be mended when the barrage stopped, but that would be done by the resident signallers.

On arrival at the top I met up with Jim Sibeon who had been joined by Lamacraft and one or two others. As we took cover in the command bunker the roof constantly shook as shells and mortars landed nearby. Sheltering with us was a young lad who had trained with us in the UK and it was apparent by his serious expression, plus his equally obvious trembling and nervousness, that he was finding it very hard to cope. We were as afraid as anyone under these conditions, but as people often do when under stress they make jokes about it. Jim and I pretended to be frightened mice ready to dig our way out with hands held chest high like paws, but our shell-shocked friend, poor lad, literally shook each time a shell landed. Nothing we could do seemed to cheer him up and I was told shortly after that he had been sent back away from the front line. Although I had never seen anyone shell-shocked in Korea, I knew what it was like because when I was an apprentice at Chester Hydraulic, I had seen an old man who was shell-shocked from the First World War.

Poor Albert Hall used to tremble uncontrollably and we used to marvel at his ability to file flat whilst his hands shook. About once every few months he would begin to shake excessively all over as he slowly started to wobble and began to sink down. Whoever was nearest would get hold of him and gently lower him down whilst at the same time calling for Alice the crane driver. (Alice was a lady crane driver who stopped on for a few years after the Second World War.) She would race the crane down the shop and make Albert comfortable, whilst at the same time taking his false teeth out. When he revived sufficiently they would sit him on a chair and give him a cup of tea, after which he would either carry on or go home. Poor Albert – can society ever repay men such as him? Knowing what shell-shock looked like I did feel concerned for our nervous friend because he was showing real signs of this disabling condition. We all felt sorry for him because no one knows how much anyone can take in such circumstances.

Finally, around teatime, the barrage ceased so that Terry and I could make our way back to our positions – how thankful we were when we eventually found ourselves sitting in our bunker enjoying a good meal. The line we had set out to repair was fixed a couple of days later, but Jim Sibeon said it was a bit of a nightmare trying to match up all the shattered cables because many of them had been shattered in several places. Terry and I decided that to avoid future breaks we would lay a completely new line to B Company, taking it through sheltered spots. The final stage up the back of Hill 355 turned out to be a mammoth task, because the cable drums were very heavy and the intense heat was unbearable. However, it turned out to be worthwhile because it did the job and we had no further problems with communications in that particular section.

Shortly after this episode an amusing incident occurred which even the best scriptwriters would find hard to dream up. On the night in question I was returning to my bunker after doing my stag on the telephone exchange, plus the task of keeping the wireless sets open. As I passed one of the mortar pits I heard the unmistakable sound of a mortar bomb sliding down the barrel. During the night the mortar lads on duty were allowed to drop a number of bombs on the enemy at irregular intervals. The idea was that it would keep the enemy in a nervous state. The lads could choose when to let the bombs go, so every now and then, just for sheer devilment, they would wait for someone coming off guard and then let a bomb go. At night the mortars gave off a long flash which, to the unsuspecting, would give a nasty shock! All good clean fun. However, on this occasion, what they didn't know was that the figure coming towards them in the dark was a Corporal Mags. As the bomb blasted off I heard the familiar sound of someone slipping and falling on the wet earth (it was drizzling that night). As the lads began to laugh the voice of Corporal Mags boomed out of the gloom – and he stuttered when he was a bit excited – 'You think – th – think, you're b – b – bloody funny, but that's your – your cup of tea gone for a Burton, s – so laugh that off!'

The next sound was that of the lads in the mortar pit whingeing, 'Oh, it was only a joke, Corp!'

'Well, the joke's on you,' came back the reply. 'You've had it!' I went to bed that night with that warm feeling you get from being privileged to a good, real-life mini-drama of the banana skin type.

As the summer progressed so the temperature rose and everything bloomed. Each day we were treated to cloudless blue skies. Everyone sported a good tan and we all set to with a will to improve our site. Bunkers, trenches, wiring and our communication lines were all upgraded to a high standard. It was at this time that Terry and I were checking out an old line when we came across a pot buried in a neglected rice field. At first we thought it might be a booby trap, but on closer inspection it was what it seemed – just an old Korean porcelain pot. But what a find! Inside were quite a number of cast bronze bowls, plus a quantity of very good blue and white pots and ornaments. They were obviously choice old pieces so we proudly took them back to our bunker and displayed them around the shelves. We even put some flowers into some, which made everyone smile. Two of the bronze bowls I kept for myself with a view to taking them home. They were to travel with me everywhere we went after that, but were destined never to belong to me permanently. When some of the older Koreans saw them they smiled, but did so with a slight shake of the head which meant they were not really ours.

Over the next two months the vases slowly disappeared one by one, and I knew that our Korean friends had won them back, but I couldn't begrudge them their treasures. After all it was their country and their artefacts, and one day we would be gone, leaving them to pick up the pieces. Now, over fifty years later, I do fully appreciate more what I had found in those far-off days. As a collector and part-time dealer in Chinese and Japanese porcelain I can recall enough to know the pieces we had found were seventeenth- or eighteenth-century pieces – maybe even earlier. The bronze bowls were, unfortunately, stolen from me on the ship which took us home. Knowing the roguish character Jones was, I suspected that there was some collusion between him and the characters I had shown them to. Jim Sibeon and I did a bit of searching for the missing items, but I never saw them again. I always regretted their loss but I suppose they were never really mine to lose. Good antiques are only held in trust and must eventually be passed on.

In the antiques trade, there is the saying 'Good antiques will eventually find their way to people who appreciate them'. In later life I was to have the pleasure of owning and selling many good Chinese and Japanese antiques. Of all life's artistic works, I have found that Chinese and Japanese ivory carvers are perhaps the best. The artistry, attention to detail and composition of the better pieces are quite amazing. Of course all art, whether in the form of painting, sculpture, music or architecture, speaks to people in a way which appeals to the finer aspects of human thought and appreciation.

Near the end of May I had two experiences which illustrate how easy it is for disaster to strike when on active service, both of which had nothing to do with the enemy. The first was to do with boiling water for shaving and washing-up purposes. We had learned during the winter that the best way to do this was to take one of the large Korean cast-iron bowls (I don't know where they got them from) and place it on a couple of pickets, then dig a small hole underneath the pickets into which we would put a small can of petrol which, once ignited along with a few sticks, would soon have the water boiling. In the early morning it would sometimes be a little bit chilly until the sun came up, so we would often stand round the open fire having a brew and chatting.

There were always plenty of 2-gallon petrol containers on site and on this particular morning I found myself standing with the back of my legs touching one. Unfortunately the spring-loaded cap could not have been closed properly, because I suddenly felt the cold rush of petrol striking my leg. The can had tipped and even as I jumped to one side the petrol ran to the fire and ignited. In a flash it zipped back and the next thing my boot was alight. I had never comprehended until that moment why people on fire often try to run away. It wasn't rational but I felt the almost uncontrollable urge to do just that. I controlled myself, however, and managed to spread my legs apart so that my other foot didn't catch alight. I was about to pull my trousers off when as if by magic a large shovel full of earth hit my foot and put the flames out. Good old 'Legs 11', our Corporal, had acted quickly and with purpose, so I was saved from what could have been a very nasty situation. 'Legs 11' was a great character who had got his nickname because his last two army numbers were 11, and in bingo this number is always called as 'Legs 11'. Luckily for me there were always plenty of shovels around the site, Legs had sized up the situation very quickly and had done the right thing. Legs was very popular with all the lads because he was always so cheerful and easy to get along with. He didn't need army type discipline to get things done because he led from the front and was always first to get stuck into any task which needed doing. Most of the time he didn't even wear his stripes, but then he didn't need to.

I had learned on my stretcher-bearer's course in the UK that danger from fire often leads to delayed shock, and so it was with me. For a couple of days after this incident I found it hard to sleep because my senses had been so hyped up that I needed time to come back down again. I recognized the symptoms so it didn't worry me too much, but there had been some quite nasty cases of injury from fire. A short time after my accident I did see one of the battalion sergeants (I can't remember his name) who had been burnt on his face, some of which looked almost second degree. He asked me what I thought and at the time I told him he should go back to the ADS for treatment. He thought about it but shook his head and decided to carry on. Two days later he was carried away on a stretcher – the delayed shock had kicked in to some effect.

As the days lengthened with the approach of summer, so the temperatures rose. On the hottest days we would be stripped to the waist with a cloth tied around our necks to wipe away the sweat. The

Koreans were not as keen as we were to strip off and they usually wore some kind of head protection. One of their best ideas was to make a hat from large sycamore leaves, and I was very pleased when Kim showed me how to do this by interweaving leaves before fastening them with twigs. They lasted a couple of days but they were very cooling whilst the leaves were still full of moisture. 'When in Rome do as the Romans do', is often good advice. Wearing head protection in hot weather is a very elementary precaution which, if ignored, can have serious consequences – and so it was with me. I had to go out on my own to mend a line which snaked back a couple of miles or so to the artillery section. I set off after breakfast, slowly working my way back towards the spot where the 25-pounders were located. As was often the case (Sod's law), the break was all but in the area of these noisy guns. By the time I had reached the artillery section the sun was up and it really was scorching hot. On the way the sun was behind me, beating down on my head and neck so that I began to feel a bit uncomfortable. I found myself frequently stopping for a drink, which was not a problem because I had my water bottle and there were a number of springs alongside the dust track road I was following. Springs were reasonably common in the area and whenever one was found the lads would sink a box in over it, lined with pebbles. Not only would this provide a 24-hour drinking fountain, but in the winter these little springs did not freeze over. Often, when the temperatures were sub-zero, you could put your hands into the water and they would feel warmer than the outside temperature. I came across several of these little outpourings and there was always a tin or a mug by the side of them so not unnaturally I had a drink and splashed my face. However, I was becoming aware that my head was aching and I didn't exactly feel with it, so to speak. By the time I arrived at the artillery section I was feeling just about all in, but I managed to mend the break I had been looking for and immediately set off to return to our mortar site. As I reached about halfway I was almost on my knees and must have covered the last half mile on auto-pilot. All I wanted to do was fall into my bunk and get my head down. I was greeted by Terry Hache and he could see I was the worse for wear. I asked him not to tell Sergeant Bingham, assuring him that I would be all right after I'd had a kip. As I flopped on my bed I heard muffled voices, but within minutes I was in dreamland. I must have slept all evening and all night because it was early morning when I awoke. My head ached but I knew I would soon be back to my usual self. Terry told me that the Sergeant had seen me and needed some persuading not to get the medics involved. However, he was reasonably assured when he saw me back in business next day.

When you're on active service the one thing you do not want is separation from your mates. Even though conditions may be harsh, the shared common hardship creates a bond which gives confidence and a certain amount of security.

Chapter 18

R&R Leave in Tokyo

As we moved into June the word spread that some of us might go on R&R (rest and recreation) leave to Tokyo. This idea seemed like a far-off dream, but we were conscious that from time to time one or two lads disappeared for a week. You had to be in Korea roughly six months before you qualified for this special treatment, but as we were to find out, it was indeed very special.

The leave was organized mainly by the Americans, who at that time were pumping large amounts of cash into Japan. It did seem rather strange that only six years earlier they had dropped the atomic bomb on the Japanese, yet here they were acting as hosts to troops fighting in Korea. Of course, the Koreans themselves hated the Japanese because of the way they had been treated when the Japs occupied their country. Even to mention the word Japanese would immediately raise the hackles of any Korean within hearing distance. In fact, some of the lads used to pretend to read one of the old newspapers which were sent to us. Then, as if they had spotted something unusual, they would say, 'Hey look at this, the Japs are getting involved.'

Any Korean who heard these comments would immediately show great concern. 'What you say? What you say?' they would exclaim. 'Number ten, number ten.'

I don't think the lads doing this realized how cruel it really was to make this type of joke. One of our more senior Koreans came up to me one day and took his shirt off to show me the scars all over his chest. He told me he had been pegged out on the ground by some Japanese soldiers after which they made little cuts all over his chest. It is an odd fact that nations who are very cultured are often the most barbaric when they go to war. Even to this day I do not think Japanese visitors to Korea are ever welcome, and I understand they are likely to get second-rate service. Old memories die hard.

Just before I went on leave to Tokyo, we were joined by a new recruit called Di Davies. He had been in the Territorial Army, but had found himself conscripted to the Welch Regiment to help make the battalion numbers up. His role was to help Terry Hache and myself, but he was a bit green so it was obvious he would need some training. Terry and I took turns in giving him advice on the wireless sets, procedures and line maintenance. A nice enough lad, he was however hard work when it came to doing things the army way. His favourite saying, in his slow, strong, Welsh accent, was, 'I know that.' Of course he didn't, but we weren't unduly worried because we knew experience would soon teach him the importance of listening to good advice.

A few days after he arrived I had reason to take him out to trace a broken line that ran in a valley which separated us from the Black Watch, or Leicesters – I was not sure which. This area was not the sort of place to hang around in because any kind of activity seen by the enemy was likely to bring down mortar or shellfire. As we entered the valley the Chinese began to shell the Black Watch who were about half a mile on our left. From where we were it was a bit like watching a film as the shells burst, but our new recruit seemed quite fascinated by the sight. I chivvied him a bit to get him moving, but in his Welsh drawl he informed me that shelling didn't bother him.

'It will,' I told him, 'when it gets close enough.'

'Oh, I don't think so,' he said.

Two degrees to the right could have easily reached us in the open with no cover, so I just ploughed ahead and got the job done.

As things would have it, the next day I was eating my dinner and sitting just inside Private Smith's bunker, when our Di came trudging up the hill towards us carrying his mess tin full of stew. As was often the case, several shells screamed overhead to land safely in the paddy fields below. To our surprise Di dived full length on the ground to land just in front of us, his dinner flung everywhere. There were several other lads with us at the time so Di was not short of sympathy.

'If you don't want your dinner tomorrow, Di, I'll eat it for you,' said one of the group. 'I didn't see you do that properly,' said another, 'can you do it again?'

As he got up, someone else said, 'I thought you liked shelling.'

Looking extremely flustered, all that our hero could say was, 'I wasn't ready for that one.'

'You never will be,' came back the reply. After that incident it was noticeable he wasn't quite as keen to say, 'I know.'

It is also worth recording that Private Smith, whose bunker we were in, was a hero of a very unusual type. He was the youngest soldier in the Battalion and, as such, he qualified for a pretty awful task related to a battalion tradition carried out on St David's Day. Poor lad, when the day arrived he was summoned to HQ where he was called upon to stand with one foot on the mess table and eat a raw leek, whilst the drummer gave a roll – something that would surely test the mettle of anyone who wasn't either blind, drunk, or one of those people who can eat red hot curry or similar. Smith took it all in good heart.

Quite suddenly, in early June, I was told to pack my bags and get ready for five days in Tokyo. A jeep whisked me back to Seoul where an old American Dakota was waiting to pick up the party I was in. And what a party it was. Someone, somewhere must have put a good word in, because when I arrived at the airport I was greeted by none other than my three best mates: Jim Sibeon, Lamacraft and MID Lewis. I don't know who worked the oracle, as they say, but God bless them, whoever it was. We were all excited at the thought of flying to Tokyo because in those days none of us had ever flown in an aircraft.

The seating wasn't exactly luxurious but we were more than glad to sit on the floor along the fuselage. During the three hours or so flight we were allowed to go into the cockpit two at time to have the instruments explained to us. We found this quite fascinating and the pilot and co-pilot seemed to enjoy our company as we bombarded them with questions, and they were very relaxed as they patiently explained how they navigated and controlled the aircraft. Little did I think then that I would see out my last ten years in industry as a Chief Safety Officer with British Aerospace, at the Kingston and Dunsfold Aerodrome sites. Home of the Harrier and the Hawk, these high-tech aircraft were a far cry from the old workhorse Dakotas.

On landing at a rather spartan airport near Tokyo, we were picked up by a Japanese coach driver who seemed hell bent on showing us how to negotiate the city outskirts without obeying any kind of road-safety considerations. Driving at high speed in his rickety old vehicle he bounced around on his seat roaring with laughter every time he had a near miss. As far as I could see the only rule of the road was that the biggest vehicle took preference and if anyone got in the way, or made you wait, you drove straight at them, honking the horn. As it happened, the padre was in our group so it wasn't long before some of the lads were exhorting him to put his hands together. At the time I couldn't make up my mind whether our madcap driver was just showing off in the cause of friendship or trying to get his own back on us for dropping the atomic bomb!

Eventually we arrived at a complex which had been used for training submarine commanders in the war. The quarters were very comfortable and well appointed with about twenty of us to each room. Everything was spotlessly clean and the meals were excellent. Every morning we would start the day with bacon and eggs and it was a real joy to sleep between clean sheets without our boots on. Showers were available and there were some large water tanks which we could swim in, so to us weary soldiers everything did seem luxurious.

The complex we were billeted in was some 8 miles outside Tokyo city centre, so on our first morning we found ourselves standing several deep on a station platform. It was a bit of a shock to see how many passengers were crammed into each carriage but compared to Korea's dusty roads, it was still comfortable travel. Once on board we soon realized we were the centre of attraction, the Japanese eyeing us with great curiosity. Some were very friendly which encouraged me to try one or two friendly Korean phrases. Big mistake. Immediately, one little old man began to talk volubly to me thinking that I could converse with him. Even when he realized I couldn't speak his language he still tried hard to make me understand that we were very welcome. When he eventually got to his station he made it clear he wanted us to come home with him. We of course politely refused but the lads found it highly amusing as they nudged me and pretended they thought that he was lining me up to meet his daughter.

On arrival in the city itself we did not know how we would be received, but we were pleasantly surprised by the polite nods and little oriental bows we received as we strolled around. My first priority was to buy a pair of shoes so that I could take my army boots off and feel a bit more civilian. Buying a pair of size 10 shoes turned out to be not only difficult, but quite amusing.

The ladies in the shoe shops I tried had very small feet (probably size 3 or 4) so that as soon as they saw mine they thought it was very funny. Giggling, they invariably brought another colleague to see what to them were monster feet. My three mates were naturally making capital out of the situation, suggesting everything about me was big! Eventually, I managed to buy a pair of size 9, but that was it. It was, however, a great feeling to once again walk in lightweight footwear on pavements and be able to look into shops. Strolling down one of the many interesting streets it wasn't long before we had the need to use our Operation Relax passes. Dressed in our summer shirts and trousers, with our Commonwealth armbands, we all had our berets pushed in our shirt lapels. Suddenly there was a squeal of brakes as an army jeep pulled up and before we could turn around two RMP sergeants jumped out. They were bristling with authority as they requested a look at our pay books and passes. As the only lance corporal in the group I acted as initial spokesman and with a friendly smile asked them what I could do for them.

'Put your hats on for a start!' snarled one.

'Now, that's not very friendly,' piped up Lewis.

The Sergeant was about to blow his top when he suddenly noticed our Commonwealth armbands and shoulder badges. 'Give me your pass book,' he growled at Lewis, so mischievous Lewis slowly withdrew his book and presented it, open at the page which had his MID recorded. The Sergeant's resolve was slowly weakening as he handed the book to his mate to read. Not wishing to lose face the Sergeant informed us in his best military style that he could charge us for not wearing our berets, but we knew, and I expect he did as well, that back in Korea our officers would just bin such a charge. At this point I think they realized it was a waste of time carrying on any conversation, especially when they saw our Operation Relax passes, and as they prepared to leave Lewis couldn't resist the temptation to have a final dig.

'What's it like in the nick round here?' he enquired, with a bland smile on his face. 'I bet it's better than being up the sharp end.'

I don't think the MPs could think of a suitable reply because they jumped in their jeep, revved up and drove off at speed with an over-the-shoulder retort, 'You'll have to watch it!'

Happily that was the last we saw of any military police in Tokyo.

Each day was an adventure as we walked the streets of this fine old city, but it was no surprise when we came across some street artists. Near the centre there were many of these hopefuls. We came across one group who were particularly keen to draw us and I thought it might be a nice memento, providing it was a good sketch. The lads impressed on the group that I was an artist so only if the portrait was good enough would we pay for it. Excitedly they told us to wait whilst they got their best man. They soon returned and I sat down on a chair in the street whilst the 'old master' got to work, but it wasn't easy to keep a pose with the others looking on. The sketch was eventually finished and I was very impressed with the quality and likeness. I paid the agreed sum of one guinea (one pound, one shilling) and we went on our way with smiles and waves from our erstwhile friends.

Tokyo of the 1950s was very impressive, but probably bears little resemblance to the city today. The railway station was a very grand affair and the Ginza shopping area was quite fascinating. I bought a number of presents to send home, as did all the lads – the lacquered cigarette boxes and gold inlaid lighters were of great quality, and the tea and coffee sets were really lovely. I bought one tea set from the American PX centre which was beautifully hand-painted with poppies.

Even in those days sending presents home was no problem because they would be parcelled and posted on the spot. Money was no problem either because we had spent hardly anything whilst in Korea so our bank balances were quite healthy. The American PX club was the equivalent of our NAAFI, but more of a de luxe model, so not unnaturally we spent quite a bit of time in it. Meals were cheap and you could purchase many items which were on sale in the Tokyo shops. You could also post parcels home from this centre, which was useful, as well as being able to get maps and advice about the city. It was whilst in this club that we finally proved that Lamacraft was a wild man of the hills. We had always pulled his leg that the place he said he came from did not exist – Abercunan. We said that they would never have caught him for National Service if he hadn't come down from the hills for a drink! When we first went into the PX club we had spied a wall-sized map of Great Britain with all towns and cities clearly marked on it. My home town Chester was there in bold letters and Jim Sibeon's Holywell was clearly marked, but guess what, no Abercunan! Jim had a job to live that one down.

Of course, for full-blooded males in Tokyo the great thing to do was to find a suitable young lady to walk out with, but the normal young Japanese ladies were most unlikely to be seen with a British soldier who was only in town for a week. The alternative was to visit the red light area and risk a dose of VD. Whilst some lads did take the risk I know many did not. Apart from the moral aspect, which was a significant factor in those days, the horrific pictures which had been shown to us during our UK training combined to discourage many lads from taking the risk. Another discouraging factor was the prevalent story that if you caught VD you would be awarded extra patrol work. Whilst this story may have sounded a bit fanciful, one of my friends who ended up in the medical service swore that he definitely knew of at least one case where this had happened. VD can become very serious and it is a fact that such cases are often progressive and can lead to other problems in later life. I had no intention of qualifying for medical help in this area of endeavour and, since there were any amount of interesting things to do and places to go and see, enjoying our five days leave was a pleasure – without recourse to the shady areas of Tokyo.

One evening, Lamacraft made the brilliant suggestion of going to a Japanese theatre, but even as we paid for our tickets something told me this was not really the best idea we had come up with. As we entered, the Japanese men and women eyed us with obvious curiosity, sometimes giving that little smile and bow that Orientals do. We did our best to nod back and smile. Taking our seats about halfway down the main aisle, we didn't know what to expect. Lamacraft had downed a few drinks before we went in so he was a bit excited and a little louder than was necessary. Jim Sibeon and I sat either side of him just in case he overdid it a bit, which as it turned out was a wise move. Once the show started we were more than a little amused by the colourful masks, clothes and sudden whoops and cries as the actors played out some fantasy. As things progressed, it became more and more difficult to tone down Lamacraft's obvious remarks and delight at the colourful, almost violent, rushes and stances of the actors. Near to the interval a particular act reached a climax where a rather buxom lady leapt at one of the men and he staggered as he held her aloft. This was also the chosen moment for Lamacraft to give a loud 'wha-hoo' at the sight of the actor tottering under her weight. Having anticipated Lamacraft's jovial reactions, Jim Sibeon and I hoisted him out of his seat and half dragged, half marched him out of the theatre. We were conscious of the many heads which turned, but the situation required action. Outside, of course, we had a good laugh but what the audience must have thought of us we could only guess. So much for Japanese culture and soldiers on leave in Tokyo.

One of the best parts of our leave was the opportunity to shower and bath every morning. Jim Sibeon and I were good swimmers so on most days we took advantage of the large tank which was available in the rest centre. We had an 18ft diving board which we used, but in reality we were of the opinion that the tank and board had originally been some kind of training tank, with the board acting as a platform to jump off, probably in full kit or something similar. Whatever its original use, we certainly appreciated its second life as a swimming pool.

All too quickly the five days came to an end, but fortunately for us our departure was put back a day due to foggy conditions at the airport. When we did at last assemble at the airport for our return journey we were all quite excited as we related our personal experiences. As we filed out to the old Dakota, there was a sudden flutter of interest as everyone turned to see two of our regulars turn up at the last minute in a taxi. Paralytic with alcohol, they staggered towards the aircraft just about able to support each other. We had been warned not to drink the local hooch, but our two friends were of the type who would not only drink it but endeavour to find the strongest brew. We all stood aside as they lurched aboard the aircraft, everyone nodding in disbelief. How can losing your marbles, making yourself ill and ending up with a blinding headache be classed as 'having a good time', especially as the characters involved would in all probability not be able to remember much about the occasion? Once on board they flopped down in a state of semi-consciousness as we sped back towards our other world.

Strange as it may seem, we were almost glad to be back with our mates, because we knew we had to finish the job we had been given and there is a certain strength in being with tried and trusted friends.

Chapter 19

The Attack, Boxing the Norfolks and Thoughts of Blighty

Once back in our mortar position, I was surprised to hear that D Company had put a full-scale attack on the Chinese positions which had been partly successful, but which had resulted in three dead and over twenty wounded. It was in this attack that Lieutenant Mennell was seriously wounded, but in spite of this he continued to lead his men until he collapsed. He was eventually half carried and half dragged in a blanket back into our lines. What a traumatic experience.

Talking to some of the lads who had been involved, they all had high praise for 'Legs 11'. Under heavy fire he had taken over one of the wireless sets and accurately directed covering fire to allow an organized withdrawal. The lads concerned told me he was very cool and calm, treating the occasion almost as if it was an exercise. Although several people gained medals for the engagement, 'Legs' was not one of them. I think that his rather non-military approach to things was probably a factor, and when I spoke to him he passed it all off as something and nothing. I am ever grateful to him for his speedy, thoughtful action when I caught fire. He was a good man to have around.

Whilst in Tokyo I had managed to buy a few long-playing records, so that when I got back I was able to play them on an old wind-up gramophone which someone had managed to acquire. One featured the songs from the musical *Showboat* and many years later, when I saw the show in London, it brought back many memories. In the evenings we would often sit in groups listening to the records, which passed many a pleasant hour and was remarkably therapeutic. Music is an international language and is definitely one of life's joys.

On occasions some of the lads would form a mock band and used to get on parade to command. Band fall in: shirts back to front, shorts bandolier fashion, oil bottles at the slope. Five or six would then come on parade dressed in all kinds of comical outfits, lining up to be inspected by whoever was in charge. The mock inspection was often hilarious as the 'acting' sergeant major passed comments and got ridiculous answers. Next, the band members would march backwards and forwards banging biscuit tin drums, tin whistles, mouth organs and playing non-existent instruments. They could also make indescribable noises with their mouths. It was highly entertaining. They would often finish their display with backward, slow marching, culminating in an inward collapse on the march. This involved the outside members of the group suddenly going very limp and leaning on the centre man as they marched off. The would-be sergeant in charge finished with a ridiculous order like, 'March towards the sea and when your hat floats, goodbye'.

It was interesting that one of the band members was a chap who really could knock a tune out on anything, be it a whistle, mouth organ, drum or whatever. But when asked how he could do it he used to shrug his shoulders and say, 'Don't know, I just can.' Having had piano lessons when I was young I knew that it wasn't guesswork which allowed him to display his talent, so when I managed to corner him and ask how it was that he had this ability he told me his father had run a dance band, so that when he was a child he had been able to play on all the instruments, as well as having music lessons.

One of the great things about National Service was this marvellous mix of people. It was a real education for all concerned and I think it gave an added dimension to the Army as it allowed great versatility.

As the summer progressed the weather got hotter, and the undergrowth blossomed and flourished so that the barren area we had arrived in soon became a semi-tropical garden. Our makeshift shower unit and the small pool were in constant use. Stripped to the waist on most days, everyone became tanned and, apart from lack of sleep, we all seemed pretty healthy. There was always lots of work to be done and we generally kept everywhere as clean and efficient as possible. The regular shelling we received ensured that there was a steady need to repair broken lines.

To some degree we got used to the shelling – that is, as far as it is possible to get used to such a thing. Our lads made sure the Chinese got their share of mortar bombs, which must have given them a hard time because our observation bunkers had got their positions well registered. In addition, English and Australian planes would strafe the Chinese positions regularly, though at times they had to face a heavy barrage as they dived in. When up with B Company I did see one of the Aussie planes get shot down and it plunged straight onto the Chinese positions. Everyone who saw it was a bit shocked. Somehow or other you expected to see the planes go in, drop their bombs and veer off, so that when one dived straight into the ground it made you realize what a desperate job being aircrew was.

Every now and then we would be treated to a firework type display on a hill about 5 miles to our right. This was the famous White Horse Hill, which was alternatively held by the Americans and the Chinese. It was said that it had changed hands twenty-nine times – a sort of 1952 version of Verdun. When the Yanks put in an assault on this particular hill it would be preceded by an almighty barrage which often lit up the sky. From what we were told they would take the hill, but after a day or so the Chinese would counter-attack and drive them off. Many people said the Chinese were only interested in the hill because they could pinch lots of American guns and supplies each time they took it. Whether there was any truth in this I do not know, but it was a fact that the Chinese were not as keen to make frontal attacks on British- and Commonwealth-held positions as they were on attacking the Yanks. Certainly it was our experience that when we took on Hill 355 and its surrounding area, the positions were in a poor state.

Whenever we took over a site it wasn't long before communication trenches were lengthened and deepened, along with other essentials like deep swill pits. Bunkers were well constructed, with great attention to detail both inside and out. Numerous slit trenches were dug all round the site so that when we were subjected to harassing fire, there was always a handy trench to dive into if we were not near a bunker. Before we left our mortar site we had slowly but surely constructed seven barbed-wire fences. This type of defence might seem outdated, but there is no doubt it is difficult stuff to traverse, especially when coiled wire is placed between each row of fences.

As we headed into July, we all became conscious that another spell in reserve was beckoning. This second time was going to be something special, because by the end of it we would only have six weeks or so before our tour of duty was over, and almost unbelievably we would be heading for home. Not long before we went into reserve we had an interesting experience when one of our lines to the 25-pounder artillery section went down, and Terry Hache and I went out to repair it.

Conforming to 'Sod's law' yet again, the break was almost on the doorstep of the artillery section, so that once we had mended the line we quite naturally stopped for a while to have a cup of tea with our gunner friends. The guns were situated on some raised ground with a road running directly underneath the forward-facing guns. Whether it was for our benefit or just coincidence I will never know, but just as we were leaving and passing under these noisy monsters, they let go a fair old salvo. I thought that the mortars were noisy but these brutes nearly deafened us and gave us a rare old start. There is no doubt anyone firing such guns for any length of time would suffer some hearing loss.

Probably for security reasons, we were never given exact dates when we would move away from Hill 355 area, but the day did arrive and in no time at all we were packing our bags and heading once more into reserve. It is hard to explain the immense sense of release which everyone felt as we boarded our vehicles to head for our temporary new home. Although only a few miles behind the line, a spell in reserve meant that we could get our heads down, relax and maybe do a bit of sport.

Holding Hill 355 and its surrounds had given everybody a hard time and it was while we were in this area that the only man in our battalion to be taken prisoner disappeared. When we went into reserve I got the full story which was indeed very unusual. It happened whilst some of our lads were on patrol well into enemy territory. From what I was told it appears that the patrol was ambushed and the unfortunate prisoner was shot before being carried off by a big Manchurian soldier. The lads in the nearest position to where the incident occurred said that they could hear him shouting for help as he was being abducted. I can't remember his name now but when the Korean War ended I did see his name as one of those repatriated. What a tale he would have had to tell. I suppose he would have been subjected to sessions of communist indoctrination, as were many prisoners taken by the Chinese in Korea, but I couldn't imagine that these sessions would bear any fruit. I did read later that wounded prisoners did not get much medical help.

Once settled in reserve, Captain Swift was soon about his business of selecting a battalion boxing team to fight the Norfolks. Jim Sibeon and I were chosen and were immediately pounding up and down the hills, plus being involved in vigorous sessions of sparring, skipping and punchbag work. Great fun. Everyone in the team fought everyone else in training, plus a few extra sparring partners, so that in no time at all we were all looking fit and ready to take on anyone. We had lost our winter weight and I was down to 11st 10lb, or thereabouts, making me a middleweight instead of a heavyweight. We knew that the match with the Norfolks was going to be no pushover so everyone set about the training routine in real earnest. No longer were the Chinese our main concern – the Norfolks were now our main target for aggression and punishment.

Whilst quite a few of the lads came along to watch us train, the Koreans, who at that time had no tradition of boxing, thought we were a very strange lot – here to fight the Chinese, yet prepared to fight each other. More than once my old friend Kim looked at me and shook his head. 'You Corporal Nev crazy!'

Our captain and best boxer was a man called Stevens, who was a very relaxed character until he got in the ring. A combination puncher, he was also a good mover and I think he could easily have made the professional ranks. I had sparred with him a few times and had enjoyed the sessions immensely. In sparring you don't usually punch your full weight, so it was hard to judge just how hard his punches were, but when we did meet the Norfolks, their captain was to find out, much to his disadvantage.

During the weigh-in the day before the actual match, Stevens had moved up to the scales in a rather laconic way, which was his wont when not in the ring. As it happened, as captain of our team, he was drawn to fight the Norfolks' captain. As Stevens stepped onto the scales the captain of the Norfolks was heard to say, 'He looks like an old man.' What a costly mistake.

As Stevens stepped back off the scales, he whispered, 'I'll make him eat those words.'

It was rumoured that my opponent was an ex-champion of Germany, but I never found out whether that was indeed the case. He gave the appearance of being fit and his nose looked as if it had taken a blow or two. Jim Sibeon was in good form and I knew anyone who got in the ring with him would know they had been in a boxing match. Come the day of the fight, we were all keyed up and ready to go. There was a good crowd from each regiment and the ring itself had been put up very professionally. Waiting to be called was the worst part as fight after fight progressed working up from the lightest weights to the heaviest. As each fight ended, points were awarded for winning and losing, the idea being that the team with the most overall points would be the final winner. Waiting in a tent near the cookhouse I was doing a few exercises when

Kim came in looking a bit worried.

'Why you fight?' he asked me. 'You could be hurt. You crazy.'

The Koreans at that time, as I have said, had no tradition of boxing, and to countrymen like Kim it really must have seemed quite mad for soldiers to come to his country, only to beat the living daylights out of each other. I could tell from the faces of the Korean spectators that they were amazed at the violence taking place in the ring. Just before I went out I gave Kim a pat on the back, but he could only shake his head and mutter, 'Number ten'. I think he was genuinely concerned for my welfare, but to me it was just an exciting occasion.

Once in the ring formalities were soon over and, anxious to get on with the job, I danced into the centre ready to test out my opponent, and tried a straight left and a right cross. To my horror I was hit by a very hard left hook which knocked me off my feet. I was more surprised than hurt as I rolled straight back up ready to get on with the fight, but the ref briefly rubbed my gloves before letting us mix it again. I had never before been knocked off my feet and this was definitely not in my script for the fight. My opponent was spurred on by this early success, but I soon blunted his fast approach with a few really hard digs. I quickly realized he was very much a counter puncher and I had to take a few hard blows to get inside. When I did land a punch I could tell he knew he couldn't take chances, but as the bell went for the end of the first round I realized he had shaved the initial exchanges.

As we came up for the second round I was well aware that I had to change the pattern of the fight and amazingly a trick taught to me by an old fitter came into my head. As a young man old Thom Leach had done some sparring with a professional boxer who had paid him to go in the ring with him because he was so fast. Thom said the professional had not taken advantage of his inexperience, but had taught him quite a few tricks so that Thom could give the professional a good workout. Thom had only met the pro boxer when he had been working away on a job and had gone to the local gym to keep fit. The trick he had taught me was to throw a hard straight left, which was designed to miss the opponent's left shoulder, but as the punch was thrown you tucked your head into your shoulder and threw a right cross over the top of your left arm. I think it's sometimes called a 'sucker punch', because your opponent sees what looks a bit like an off-balance left cross but doesn't see the right cross coming over your left arm.

As we came out for round two I sparred up and threw my left hand as described, then followed it up with a full-blooded right cross. It couldn't have worked better. My opponent caught my right full force on his jaw. I knew I had really hurt him because he paled slightly and immediately began to back pedal. I went after him throwing combination punches right and left, many of which landed, although none as decisively as the right cross. It was obvious by the way my opponent covered up and used the ring that he had spent a lot of time in a boxing ring. Towards the end of the round he recovered his composure and we exchanged some hard blows before the bell went. If the first round was his, this round was mine. I knew winning the fight depended on this last round and I was fairly sure that I carried a slightly heavier punch than my opponent, which forced him to carry on trying to lure me into situations where he could counter punch. About a minute before the end of the last round we went into a clinch and I suddenly remembered a move Corporal Oram had taught me which at the time seemed worth a go. Just as we were about to break I nudged my opponent with my shoulder, throwing him slightly off balance and then gave him a good dig in the ribs. I was just congratulating myself when the ref pulled us apart and told me I was not allowed to make such a move. Corporal Oram had taught me a professional trick which wasn't allowed in amateur boxing.

Although I put in a vigorous finish I was pretty sure this caution had lost me the fight, because there wasn't a lot in it at this stage. Sure enough my opponent was given the verdict but when we were presented with our cups later, the senior officer making the presentation praised us both for a close, hard-fought fight.

By the time we came to the last bout of the tournament, both teams were equal on points, and by coincidence this was between the team captains, who were the best boxers in the contest. The Norfolk man was good but Stevens was at his best and by the end of the third round his opponent was literally out on his feet. He put up a brave performance but after the fight he couldn't get up off his stool – he was literally punched out. That evening we had a great party in one of the bell tents, during which I met my opponent and we had a drink together. Everyone enjoyed themselves, several of the lads giving a song or two. The officers and NCOs all joined in and Captain Swift was well pleased with the result. He went round congratulating the lads, patting everyone on the back and dishing out praise. He was a most likeable character, always encouraging his lads in a quick but sincere way, yet always ready for a joke.

I never fought a competitive fight after the one described because once I got back to civvy street, football and athletics were my first choice. However, later in my life, when I became an apprentice instructor in a training workshop, I was able to take the apprentices on twice-weekly, two-hour physical training sessions during which I included the elements of boxing, punchbag and speed skipping. The lads used to enjoy the sessions, especially when I invited them to hit me as hard as they could, while I demonstrated the art of self-defence. Boy, did they try!

After our match with the Norfolks we had a visit from the world-famous boxer Jimmy Wilde who at that time must have been in his sixties or seventies. What a marvellous sportsman he was. In his heyday he fought well over a 100 fights, only losing two or three, and quite often he had to give weight away to get a decent fight. When Bruce Woodcock was challenging for world honours in the late 1940s Jimmy was the only boxing reporter to write that he thought the fight with Joe Baxi should not take place. In the event his warnings proved to be right because Baxi broke Woodcock's jaw. Better handling and training of Woodcock at that time might well have turned him into a world champion.

Jimmy Wilde was given a great reception by the lads when he came to speak to us, and after he had finished telling some fascinating stores he invited the audience to ask him any questions. I asked him the obvious one. For such a slim, lightweight man, where did he get his knockout punch from? As I expected, he said that if there was a secret it was timing, and I am sure he was right. Timing is the essential element in all sports and I knew from my own experiences in football that when you volley a ball and the timing is right, it feels right and the ball flies from your boot with an unstoppable force. A sportsman like Jimmy was an inspiration to us lads in those far-off days. We really did appreciate his effort in travelling 12,000 miles to speak to us in what was then a little-known country. I am sure Jimmy would have made a success of whatever he did, and in many ways his visit to us represented what this conflict was about – the ability of people to make a free choice, regardless of their wealth or position.

Our spell in reserve soon passed and it seemed that in no time at all we were again being loaded into trucks to head for what should be our last spell in the line. The weather in September was very good, but beginning to get nippy at night as the dreaded winter approached.

*

Our new position was on some low-lying hills which formed a U-shape. We were to be positioned at the bottom of the U, which placed us a mile and a half or so from the Chinese. With binoculars you could see their movements, but we felt that they were far enough away not to be too much of a threat compared to our previous position.

The Aussies we were taking over from were a great bunch of blokes. Good soldiers, but rather laid back compared to the British Army. They were slightly amused when we started tidying up the communicating lines and sorting out the bunkers. To our surprise many of the Aussies were Englishmen who had gone out to Australia on the £10 immigration scheme.

The scheme was launched in the late 1940s to allow people to emigrate to Australia for a fare of just £10. As it turned out 'all that glitters is not gold' was the sad experience for many who accepted the challenge. On arrival in Australia a lot of the people involved were held in placement camps before being offered very unacceptable types of work. The result was that for those who wanted to go back home, the only way to raise enough money was to join the Australian Army. Whereas we were paid £1 10s per week, the Aussies were paid the same amount per day. In the three or four days we were with the Aussies, we were constantly bombarded with questions about Blighty and, similarly, we were all particularly interested in meeting anyone from our town or village. During conversations I heard the name Teddy Ferguson mentioned which was rather exciting because, from descriptions given, it was almost certain the Teddy Ferguson I had known in my youth.

Teddy (not Edward) was one of a large family who had lived on the same estate as I, and although they were poor, they were all nice children. Up to the age of about fourteen years, Teddy and I were firm friends and would roam the fields where we lived, enjoying the countryside. We often used to wrestle together until one of us got a fall or submission. Wrestling was a regular pastime of lads in those far-off days, but because my cousin was a professional wrestler I was usually up to date with the latest holds and counter-holds, many of which I can remember to this day. As soon as I found out Teddy was only a mile or so away, I got Terry Hache to cover for me whilst I set off to find him. Was this to be our 'Stanley-Livingstone' moment?

As I reached the Aussie positions where Teddy apparently was, I was stopped by a guard on the road. As soon as I explained what my mission was, he took me to his Sergeant who told me that the Teddy Ferguson I was looking for was definitely in their company, but that sadly he had left by truck about an hour earlier. As was the Aussie way, the Sergeant insisted I join them for a drink and we spent a pleasant hour swapping stories, but then it was time for me to return to my own unit.

I remember talking to one cockney soldier who was in the Australian Army and he said that nearly all the British contingent were men who had accepted the £10 scheme, but had become disillusioned on arrival. They really felt the government had conned them, as indeed they had.

I was very disappointed at not finding my friend and as I walked back my mind returned to those sunshine days when I had wandered around the countryside near Chester, played endless hours of football, cricket, roller skating, swimming in the River Dee, and all the other seasonal pursuits now forgotten by modern youth: cigarette card games, conkers, bowl hoops, pie crust and many more.

Our changeover period with the Aussies went all too quickly because they were very excellent company and we had some good laughs as we exchanged stories and generally got bedded in. From what they told us, the positions we had taken over were usually quite quiet, but as Terry Hache and I were to find out, this did tend to breed a feeling of false security.

After a couple of weeks of getting our positions sorted out to our usual standard, we felt we could relax a bit and for the first time since we had entered the war we began to believe that going home was a real possibility. A lot of us were due to be demobbed in January, and it had been said that the maximum time you could be expected to stay in Korea was twelve months. We were now within six or seven weeks of the date we had arrived, which was about 11 November 1951.

Cold at times, the weather was bright and clear, and we seemed to have plenty of time on our hands. One particular morning, Terry Hache and I had finished our early duties so we thought we would have a stroll to the top of the hill to look across the valley to the Chinese positions. Suddenly, as we stood on the brow (something you should never do), a stream of bullets whistled just overhead. You don't need to be told to get your head down when this happens, but we were very surprised because we had assumed the Chinese were that bit too far away to be a real danger. Big mistake! How stupid can you be? Here we were, two experienced soldiers making the most elementary mistake like that of a raw recruit – standing on the skyline facing the enemy. Needless to say, my father's words of warning came back sharply to me.

To make life easier with regard to tracing telephone lines, Terry and I had developed the simple system of erecting a pole outside our bunker, to which all our lines were attached, each one being neatly tied and labelled. This meant that if we had to trace a line which had been broken we could easily pick up the start of the line. Once we had organized our lines properly, we decided to trace each one to its destination so that in the event of a breakdown we would have a good idea of where it went, even in the dark. To this end I decided one morning to trace one of our lines to B Company, which was probably three-quarters of a mile away. All went well until I got to within about 50yds of the position. At this point the line went through several layers of wire fence, but there was no scrambled wire in between, so they were not difficult to negotiate, and I didn't feel like doing a big detour to reach our signals lads in their command bunker.

Ducking under the wire, I had not gone many yards into the long grass when there was an ominous 'click' as my leg struck a tripwire. As I froze to the spot all kinds of hair- raising thoughts flashed through my mind. Had I set off a mine? Was this the end? A split second later a flare went off just to my left, but whilst this gave me some relief it didn't prove that I was not in a minefield. Gathering my thoughts I decided to do what we had been trained to do in such circumstances. Using the butt end of my rifle, I cautiously moved forward watching each step warily as I gently probed ahead for more wires. Tripwires are set at about a 7lb load so if you are very careful you can touch them without setting them off. Slowly I inched forward apprehensively cutting each wire that I found. After what seemed an eternity, I eventually arrived at the last fence and I can remember the utter feeling of relief as I made my way towards the command bunker.

On reflection, I had made a big mistake going into the wired area, but our Battalion had not made use of flares in wired areas, because the CO was of the opinion that if used they might illuminate the enemy but might also gave a clear view of our positions. Since we were obviously more aware of our location than the enemy, the CO believed that to light up the area was to the enemy's advantage. Unfortunately, other units took a different view and I was told that the Canadians, who had held these positions before the Aussies, had laid the flares. It was said that they had also laid some mines, but there was no record of where they had been put. The line I had been following must have been laid, therefore, prior to the wire fence being erected, but one thing was for sure, I wouldn't be following it along that route again!

When I entered the bunker, my signals mates thought it was a bit of a joke for me to have got trapped within the wired area. Their attitude was that as it was only three or four weeks to go before we were to be sent to reserve well behind the line, together with the likelihood of heading for home, they were going to do as little as possible. After those two hair-raising incidents I decided that it was time I, too, eased off, and so I did.

Shortly after, I was told to report to one of the captains in another company with a view to acting as his signaller on some training exercises for the newly arrived troops. The Captain was one of the marshals of the mock battles and I was able to enjoy three or four days of walking by his side, my job being to pass messages from the Captain to the Directing Staff. I've forgotten his name but he was easy to get on with and I found that my 33 Set was very adequate for the terrain. Woods and hills would often interfere with the old equipment, which had a range of about 3 miles. However, on this exercise the Captain and I were mostly positioned on vantage points so that he could analyse what was going on and the radio received and transmitted at strength five.

Every time we stopped to have a bite to eat and drink, the troops who were undergoing training would come over to enquire what it was like to be up at the front. Their nervousness was easy to understand, but after nearly a year in Korea I was surprised at how hardened and accepting we had become to life in that theatre of war. We lived in holes in the ground, and our minds and bodies had become used to the daily grind. There were no flat areas in Korea, except the paddy fields. Everywhere we went was up or down hill. We had become expert at recognizing the scream of incoming or outgoing shells, and our never-ending night duties became a norm. Consequently, when I was asked what it was like, I could only give a fairly stock answer, such as, 'Keep five rounds in your magazine. Make your bunker as strong and as good as you can, with plenty of rocks on top. Keep yourself clean and keep your head down when the shelling starts. Good luck!'

A few days later we got our marching orders to abandon life at the front and head across the Imjin River to a campsite some 30 or so miles distant. On arrival, we were given bivouac tents and told to settle in for about a week. We were mixed in with some freshly arrived troops and were amazed at how careless they were in setting up their tents and storing their kit. As soon as we had got our tents and flysheets up we dug little trenches all around the edges of the tent in case it rained. Having water flow through a tent is not really a good idea. The new lads, on the other hand, thought we were being over-fussy with our preparations, but their attitude changed when it began to rain heavily.

During the day we were able to use marquees which had been erected specifically for meals and recreation, so that was a positive step. Night-time, however, was a different matter. Our tents held all right, and we were particularly careful not to touch the sides when wriggling in and out, but these inexperienced troops seemed to think this didn't matter and consequently it wasn't long before many of them were suffering the agonies of incessant dripping on them and their gear.

About two days after the rain started, Terry Hache and I were gently dozing when at about 0500 hrs some faces appeared through the flap of our tent. Wet and very miserable, two of the replacement troops had begun to learn important basic lessons. Their tents were completely waterlogged, all due to their carelessness. Any experienced camper knows that if you let anything touch the sides of a tent when it is wet, the water will enter at that point. Either the lads weren't aware of this, or just didn't care, but they looked a sorry sight as they pleaded to be allowed into our tent. We could afford to be magnanimous at this stage of our army careers because we knew we only had days to go before we began the long-awaited journey to Seoul and then Pusan. Under pain of being thrown out if they so much as nutted our tent, we allowed them to squeeze in and lay still whilst we got a brew going. Once they had had a drink and a bite to eat, their spirits began to revive, and they could see the funny side of their predicament. Quite naturally, Hache and I were two of the best blokes they had ever met. Apparently they had become soaked at about 0200 hrs and had spent the next three hours trying to get sorted out before they gave up and squelched over to our tent. Recounting their pathetic endeavours made them see the funny side of their self-inflicted misery. They struggled to dig some gulleys in the dark, whilst all the time getting wetter and wetter. And, of course, they cursed and blamed each other for the situation they were in. It all added up to valuable experience and doubtless an anecdote for the folks back home.

As we prepared for our final move from this temporary camp I decided to seek out Kim and Chan to say a final farewell. On enquiry I found that a dozen or so of the porters, including my two firm friends, were gathered in one of the larger 12ft bell tents, but the atmosphere was very sombre as I entered. In my excitement at the thought of leaving for home, I had paid no heed, until this precise moment, to the fact that it was a sad occasion for our porters. Many of them had been serving the war effort before we arrived and would have to continue long after we had gone. No wonder they were feeling sad. We had formed a close bond with them and they had taught us much about living in this harsh climate. Their unflinching loyalty, honesty and unremitting hard work was beyond calculation. These were truly 'gentle-men'. As I shook hands with each of them I, too, felt a great sadness at leaving such good friends. I gave my lumberjack boots to Kim, which he accepted with a broad smile, but I was very conscious that all I could really give was my respect and good wishes. Their simple, 'You OK, Corporal Nev,' was worth more than any medal. Even now, over fifty years later, I can truthfully say I have never met better men than those Korean porters and I have often wondered what their fate was.

After the short stay under canvas, we were shepherded back to a transit camp near Seoul, from where we were to be taken to Pusan to board the old troopship Devonshire. As we headed further and further away from the front line an extraordinary feeling took hold of us. The very idea of 'going home' was dreamlike – and everyone became a little nervous at the thought that something might happen which would delay us. If the Chinese made a big push would we be sent back up the line? Was there really a ship ready to take us home?

Years later, as a volunteer prison visitor, the experience of leaving Korea enabled me to appreciate what prisoners called 'gate fever'. When long-term prisoners were due for release they often used to get so anxious that they might lose their remission, they would report sick to try and get into the hospital. It was said that some would even harm themselves so that they could get out of the prison area into the hospital.

When we arrived in Pusan, quite a number of the lads were in this anxious state, desperate not to let anything happen to stop them getting on the boat. One of my mates, who had the same name as me, asked me whether I knew anything about rashes. What was he concerned about rashes for? I asked him. It then transpired that some of the lads had been spreading the rumour that when you had your final medical check before leaving, if you had a rash they would keep you back. Cruel joke, but Will had taken it seriously and was genuinely worried about not being able to board with the rest of us. I did my best to reassure him that this wasn't the case, but he was so wound up about it he asked me if I would have a look and give him an opinion. There was no placating him so we posted a sentry – two men in a toilet block were likely to result in us both missing the boat if we got caught! – and went into a toilet to have a look However, on inspection, I convinced him that there was nothing to worry about, but this incident does show just how anxious men can get when they are due to be taken out of a war zone, whereas whilst you are serving in it you almost subconsciously adapt to the way of life demanded by the situation.

Before we boarded *Devonshire*, Jim Sibeon and I had an amusing experience whilst stationed at the transit camp just outside Pusan, from where we could see the sea, which looked to be about half a mile away. Jim and I were both good swimmers so we decided to go to the coast and see if we could have a dip. As it turned out it was a bit further than we thought and as we got nearer we were surprised to see some Korean women collecting seaweed on what was a rocky shoreline. Fear not, press on regardless, we resolved, as we stripped off and put our shorts on to have a dip. When the ladies saw our hairy chests they went into fits of giggles. If my memory serves me right, we heard them say 'Tajy' which means 'bear'. Korean men tend to be hairless on their bodies, so I suppose we were a bit of a curiosity. Not deterred, we dived into the sea, but it was very cold and there seemed to be seaweed everywhere. We didn't stop in very long, but I think the ladies found it very amusing.

On a more serious note, before we finally left Korea we had to attend a memorial service at the Pusan war graves cemetery. There is something unreservedly sad about war graves. Row after row of neat graves, each with the name of a soldier, who in most cases was only a young man. Not for them a full life, and no doubt an everlasting void in some mother's, father's or brother's heart. Jim Sibeon, Lamacraft and I looked for the graves of mates we had known and I found it very heart-searching looking at those small white gravestones. This was particularly so in the case of Corporal Oram. When you have exchanged leather with someone in the boxing ring, you often develop a respect and real kinship. It was he who had taught me all I knew about the noble art and we had had many a good set to. But he had foretold, just before we landed in Korea, of his own premature death, and thus I had lost a good friend. Privates Rowe and Harris had also been good mates, all of which made the memorial service a sad affair. Poor men – to die in a country so far from home, what must their families have gone through?

After a couple of trips into Pusan we were easily convinced that nothing had changed. That vision of children begging in the streets has stayed with me all my life and I have, and always will, contribute to the Save the Children Fund. In any war children always suffer the most and have no way of helping themselves to a better life without adult help and encouragement. But it is a quite a magical thing that even in the worst conditions children will conjure up smiles and be happy if shown the slightest bit of love and attention.

Chapter 20

Home, Everlasting Love and Lessons for Future Generations

It seemed almost surreal as we boarded *Devonshire*, and the trip home was a delight – no enemy, no guards, as much sleep as we wanted, good food and all the time in the world to relax. Jim Sibeon, Lamacraft, Jim Swarbrick and I all volunteered for duty as deck orderly, which again meant we could go ashore at each port of call. There was no boxing but we had a tug-of-war competition which our company won. Tug-of-war is a strange sport. To the spectator it looks as if nothing is going on, but to the participants it is absolutely energy sapping and very good fun.

What a real treat it was to wander the streets of Hong Kong once we had crossed the China Seas, yet we were not entirely sure we were truly on our way home until we left Hong Kong harbour. Somewhere in the back of our minds there was the uneasy thought that something big might blow up in Korea, and we would have to turn around and head back. What a thought!

It was also a delight to call in once again at Singapore, Colombo and Aden, before entering the Mediterranean, although we were very unprepared for the gales that hit us as we sailed through this normally calm, blue haven of peace and quiet. But if it was rough in the Mediterranean, it was nothing to what met us as we entered the sea off the coast of Spain. Hurricane force winds of 100mph tossed the ship around, causing the propeller to come out of the water. This made the boat shudder from end to end and the vibration didn't exactly make one feel confident that the journey was altogether as safe as one would have liked.

Looking out to sea one day, I remember catching sight of a small fishing boat about a quarter of a mile away, bobbing on the sea like a cork. It would alternatively appear battling through a giant wave and then literally disappear out of sight as it plunged into the trough of the wave

– they are brave men, indeed, who go to sea in small boats.

We lost five days sailing between Gibraltar and the Isle of Man. Devonshire ploughed and rolled its way across the Bay of Biscay, sometimes creaking and groaning like a giant in pain. People got thrown about and our never-been-seasick Lamacraft had to make for the toilets to throw up, accompanied on each side by some of the lads jeering him on. He had made a point of cheering on some of our seasick mates on the way out, so quite naturally they returned the favour. 'Get it up, lad!' they urged as the boat lurched and rolled. So bad was the weather that we spent three days doing figures of eight around Anglesey and the Isle of Man. Everyone was so anxious to dock and go home that rumours about whether the pilot had come aboard were rife. Eventually the weather eased and we sailed in to Liverpool.

Crammed onto the quayside were hundreds of anxious families waiting to see their loved ones. Wives, sweethearts, mothers, fathers, friends – what a sight! What a joy to see my parents again and to step once more onto the soil of good old England. Bronzed by the weather, I think we must have looked a fairly healthy lot, but the first thing that struck me as we manoeuvred into the harbour was the pale, careworn faces looking up at us. Sailing in behind us was the magnificent *Empress of Canada*, which was a luxury liner. Amazingly, two weeks later she caught fire and turned turtle in the dock, a fact which we read about in the newspapers, but found it hard to believe.

It was a truly wonderful feeling to be home again and as I walked down the gangplank I saw our much-respected Captain Swift. Looking across he waved and said, 'Keep it up, Williams!' I think he meant my boxing, but whatever his meaning it was nice to wave goodbye to my favourite officer – a real gentleman.

We had to pass through customs, of course, but they weren't really interested in us. As we broke into various groups we shook hands with some of the friends we had made in other battalions, and in no time at all we were whisked away and loaded onto trains to be taken to Maindy Barracks in Cardiff. On arrival at Cardiff station we were met by a fleet of trucks – who should be in charge of the one Jim Sibeon, Lamacraft and I were to board but my old officer and friend, Lieutenant Mennell. What a shock it was to see this once effervescent soldier now diminished to a shadow of his former self. I knew he had been shot up, but I had only vaguely heard that he had been depressed, or perhaps shattered might be more accurate. I was really shocked to see how badly he had been hurt both physically and mentally. His face was gaunt and he moved slowly, almost trancelike, and barely recognized me as he tried to smile when I shook his hand. This lovely man had indeed paid the price of war. It was sad, sad, sad.

After a few days in Cardiff we were given a train pass and were soon on our way home. It was the simple things which gave us the greatest pleasure on our return: the marvellous feeling it gave me when I walked down a street full of brightly lit shops, even in those austere days, full of things to buy; walking on flat pavements and not having to do a week's night duty; sleeping between clean sheets with my boots off, and pleasing myself what I wanted to do and when to do it; sitting with friends in a café sipping coffee at my leisure or going to dances to meet some girls again, and getting my running spikes out again. Everything we had taken for granted before going to Korea was now a fresh discovery and much more appreciated.

After our Christmas leave we had to return to Cardiff to see out a couple of weeks prior to demob. Quite naturally the permanent army staff at the barracks didn't want us contaminating new intakes so they gave us huts which were tucked away in the corner of the barracks. No one seemed to know what to do with us so we were free to roam around the city and generally please ourselves. Before being handed our final discharge papers, we had one amusing incident which is worth recounting.

Lamacraft, Jim Sibeon and I were at a loose end one afternoon, so we asked one of the sergeants if there were any jobs he wanted doing. He thought for a moment then told us to follow him. We were taken to a remote section of the barracks that we hadn't seen before which resembled what can only be described as a yard in a stable block. Various bits of equipment were dotted around, so we wondered what we had volunteered for.

'Right, lads,' he said, 'you can do me a favour and generally tidy up this junk.' Then, as an afterthought, he pointed to a huge tree stump, which must have been 6ft in diameter and added, 'When you've finished you can chop that up – if you feel like it. The squaddies would like to see it go. It's their punishment tree. They have to try and chop some of it up if they've committed an offence.'

'Right Sarg, leave it to us,' we all sang out in unison.

What a joke! Once the Sergeant had disappeared we set to with a will using Kim's tree-chopping technique. Working from the outside in, we soon split the tree into four sections using wedges and axes. Following the grain and concentrating on areas of the tree which gave least resistance, we methodically divided the timber into smaller and smaller sections. Hearing all this intense activity, one or two of our mates strolled over and when they saw the fun we were having joined in as well, so that after only a couple of hours of hard graft we had this very large stump reduced to neat bundles of firewood. We brushed and cleaned an area inside the stable section, then stacked the wood in neat piles, as one would see on the Continent against the side of alpine cottages, Tyrolean style. This gave us just enough time to have a cup of tea before the Sergeant returned. He started by thanking us for our cleaning efforts, but then he suddenly realized the tree trunk had gone. Keeping my face straight I explained that we had done exactly as he suggested and chopped it up. At first he couldn't believe it, but when we showed him the wood stack he was amazed. Ruefully, and with grudging admiration, he agreed that we were more than useful with an axe.

Two years to the day after I was conscripted I was given my release papers, along with just enough kit to do my two years' compulsory Territorial Army service, which involved some half-dozen weekends and one two-week camp. I arrived home on a Thursday and started work back in engineering the following Monday.

At the time many people asked why I hadn't taken a longer leave. How could I explain what a pleasure it was to be back to a normal life after what I had experienced living in a hole in the ground for all those months. I had always enjoyed my work but now it was something special. To be paid a reasonable wage for doing something I liked doing after being in a war not of my own choosing, was indeed a pleasure and a privilege. There was also the chance to carry on my studies at night school three times a week, though some people would have called it hard work. Not in my book, because I knew the qualifications would lead to opportunities in the future, as indeed they did.

There was also the joy of kicking that piece of leather called a football after two years with hardly a game. There was the pleasure of athletics with Wirral Harriers in the summer, where I was moderately successful, and made some good friends training and running with the club. The quarter mile was my favourite event, the highlight being when I won the club championship. However, athletics was only a means of keeping fit for the football season, which it did to the extent that when I played in semi-professional football with Pwllheli in the Welsh League, and later with Northwich in the Cheshire League, I could more than hold my own, though I kept my amateur status. Amateur, that is, not counting the £5 I found in my football boot. Even when I had a week's trial with Manchester United where I could pit myself against great players like Tommy Taylor and Duncan Edwards, I was equally as fit as they were.

Two years after National Service I was forced out of the game by injury, but as the saying goes, as one door shuts, another one opens – and so it was for me. At that time I met the girl of my dreams and now over fifty years later we are still as much in love as we were then, in fact more so. We are blest with three fine sons, all of whom are happily married, and are grandparents to three super boys and two lovely granddaughters. We had a beautiful daughter, but sadly she died when only fourteen. Born with a heart condition, which was inoperable, she was a great joy to us. In her short life she taught us much about courage and love, such that my wife and I still feel her presence.

The fifty plus years I have spent since those far-off days in Korea have been packed with experiences both high and low, but many of the lessons I learned in that war-torn country have proved a useful sounding board. In concluding my story I would like to share my views on war.

Lessons to be Learnt

War is a terrible thing. Once started no one knows when it will end. It is only fought by young men, but almost invariably it is started by older men.

It can, in a strange way, bring out both the worst and the best in men and women, and although it is negation of life, for it seeks to destroy rather than build, yet not infrequently its horrors cause people to turn to God and find true religion.

In my case it happened before I left for Korea when I was given that small booklet in which was printed 'The Sermon on the Mount'. During the long night watches I read this great work and suddenly I found the words were almost jumping off the page. Since those days these great words of wisdom have been my guiding light. They have never failed me and I know they will carry me to life's end, because the words in this text are life's true foundations. When considered carefully they will always point the way to the right decisions in life. They do not always offer the easy way, but certainly the right way.

When I landed in Korea as a young National Serviceman, I felt that I was there to fight for an ideal, which was that of living in a freely elected society, as against the communist doctrine which placed the state above and out of reach of the individual. Communism, at that time, was spreading its tentacles far and wide, seeking to dominate any country which didn't, or couldn't, oppose it. It was, in my book, a 'Bully Boy'.

I had no dislike of the Chinese, but since they were the enemy then it followed we would at least have to resist them, and in the worst case attack them. My own personal view was that since I had been drawn into this war for a limited period, then survival was the number one priority and I would do everything I could to survive. I would also do everything I could to help my mates survive.

Even in those far-off days I was of the opinion that communism was a stupid illusion which would eventually collapse inwardly. The idea that people are equal or can be made equal is a fallacy of life. Everyone is a unique individual and though we may have many common needs, as well as a need to have laws which allow a well-regulated society, we are in no way equal. Even the laws we need to govern and regulate society need to be administered with deep thought and understanding. Might we say 'wisdom'?

My limited experience of war was enough to make me realize what my father and his generation went through in the First World War. Their sufferings were of such gigantic proportions that many of the men involved could not talk about their experiences, and even to think about those days would bring tears to their eyes. It is so very sad that the great opportunities created by these men are squandered by many of the modern generation. When I was demobbed in 1953, several of my football and athletic friends who had been in the Second World War gave me some insights into their experience. One particular friend had been in the Argyle & Sutherland Highlanders as a sergeant and was involved in the Normandy landings. He said that after a couple of weeks of combat you were so hungry and weary that you could easily have shot anyone who caused you danger or aggravation, including your own officers. With regard to prisoners, they had been told not to take any, but just press on. When six Germans gave themselves up my friend, being a sergeant, discussed with one of his corporals what to do. The Corporal suggested that the situation should be left in his hands. A few minutes later there was some Sten gun fire from behind a haystack and the problem was solved. Barbaric? Against the Articles of War? How can you rationalize? Very often in war the first casualties are the standards you are fighting for. Only the victors talk about war crimes. Where do you draw a line in war? How can a shell or a bomb differentiate between women and children?

In any war, children are perhaps the cruellest victims of conflict, especially after the war is finished, and many are left maimed or orphaned, to fend for themselves. Korea was left with a massive problem of orphaned children after the war, with alarming levels of tuberculosis spreading across the country. But who picked up the pieces? The Save the Children Fund played a major role, but sadly the governments involved did little to solve the problem. It is my belief that any society which ill-treats its children is, in the long run, sowing the seeds of conflict. There is no doubt that war feeds on fear, want, pride, arrogance and society's inability to deal with bullies, whether individually or collectively.

In this area of human endeavour everyone has a part to play in preventing bullies from gaining advantages over reasonable and decent people. Whether at work, home, or play –whether in politics, industry or commerce, bullying must be resisted. To oppose the disruptive force of bullying often requires courage of the highest order, but to turn away from this type of arrogance, without opposing it, is to sow the seeds of war. There is no doubt that people in positions of power have a great responsibility in preventing conflict, but all too often power corrupts those in possession of it. 'Whoever shall be the master of all, shall be the servant of all,' was the wise advice which Christ gave, but how often do those in power adopt this life-giving principle? It is much easier to demand that you have your own way in life than to ask for it with grace and patience. It is easier to be unforgiving than forgiving. War always demands an unrelenting, unforgiving nature.

The Chinese I fought against in Korea were only conscripted soldiers like myself, who in ordinary times would be friendly and no doubt well disposed towards me and any other people they might meet or do business with. In fact, I have a great regard for the Chinese. Their tenacity, artistry and ability to work hard make them a powerful nation. Who, for instance, ever heard of a Chinese immigrant bemoaning his lot? No! They just roll up their sleeves and get on with life. Although the Chinese are classed as communists, I believe they have moulded the ideology to suit their needs and in some ways they still live under an Emperor-type regime. Chinese everywhere are great survivors and in

Korea suffered a great deal of punishment that would have made other nations retreat or give in.

One of the enigmas of our time is the fact that the more technically developed nations become, the more fearsome and destructive their weapons become. When the atomic bomb was developed, Britain and America announced that only they would have it. In what dream was that announcement thought of? Not only have other nations now got the bomb but there is no doubt that once developed, if the bomb can be used, it will be used. The developers of these would-be destroyers make the excuse that these devilish devices are just for defence. My own view of this ghastly phenomenon is that I would rather have one dropped on me than be the one to use one on someone else. This, and other horrific weapons, is a Pandora's box, and unless the nations can learn to live together, then eventually they will perish together.

The great moral question we have to face now is: should any nation possess these monsters, or be allowed to invent further planet-destroying weaponry. The growth of germ warfare is obscene and the majority of people in the world would abhor such developments.

My experience of life tells me that there is a common bond running through humanity such that if you smile, a smile will come back to you. Love and kindness are appreciated and prized amongst all people, but it is the power-seekers, bullies and those who covet another's possessions who despoil life – the raised fist, the harking back to ancient wrongs.

The way we care for each other is a true measure of society, but quite often silver-tongued politicians paint false and unrealistic pictures of how life is or could be, so that individuals and even nations are led astray.

'By their fruits ye shall know them. You do not gather grapes of thorns,' were wise words Christ spoke, which are as true today as ever they were. Dishonesty is another friend of war so that I think it is true to say a good society is one that values the truth.

If we bring up our children with the correct values and attitudes, I believe the future can be bright, but if through self-seeking, neglect and lack of care for our young, we allow life to become undisciplined, and without a firm moral base, then as the good book says: We will reap what we sow.

That there will be wars and rumours of war is almost certainly true, but as individuals and as a nation we can minimize the disease of war, especially if we recognize the symptoms: a lust for power, greed, self-seeking, arrogance, bullying and the worship of money, science and pleasure. Man-made ideologies which do not recognize God are sure to fail, because in our short lives we can only ever recognize a small part of the order and meaning of life, but we do instinctively recognize the values of true love, in all its forms.

Education can help people live more useful or purposeful lives, but of itself it does not make us more thoughtful or moral. The great truths as contained in such works as 'The Sermon on the Mount' are the rudiments of life which speak to the heart and allow individuals to live with grace and purpose.

Is there such a thing as a righteous war?

If there is, it is about defending ourselves, women and children, against an aggressor or unwanted intruder. Maybe an uninvited bully who covets that which is ours by birthright or hard-worked possession.

War is a negation of life and a rage against nature which often robs the flower of youth of their place in the world, which is cruel and unfair in the extreme.

As never before the world now stands on the edge of a precipice gazing down at destructive forces of unimaginable terror, and unless these beasts of war are chained then civilization as we know it may come to an end.

Everywhere there are signs of aggression as the more technically advanced nations plunder the natural resources of the poorer countries. Speed and greed are the driving forces behind the decimation of the planet and, whilst everyone can blame governments, I believe that each and everyone of us has a crucial part to play in trying to be more thoughtful, honest and caring, not only for the planet, but our fellow human beings. A reverence for life in all its forms will give us life, but the raised fist, the thoughtless or cruel act, can only bring despair and war.

'By their fruits ye shall know them!'

As we progress in the twenty-first century, all the signs point towards a war to end all wars. With climate change bearing down on us, can the more advanced countries be persuaded to draw back from their thoughtless use of the basic materials which support life on this magnificent planet?

As water, wood and the various ores and fuels get used up, so will the pressures to share grow. The basic problems we now face nearly all come from our desire to want more and more of the goods and services supplied by the two great forces of science and technology, but science and technology have no spiritual or moral component in their make-up. They are just the study and use of 'what is'! Therefore, unless there is a great spiritual and moral awakening, science and technology, allied to speed and greed, will continue to decimate this unique and blessed planet. If we do not meet this challenge then we will not only have terrible wars, but the future for our children will be obliterated and life as we know it will cease to exist.

If only people fought as hard for peace as they do for war!